On Prayer and Meditation

On Prayer and Meditation

St. Peter of Alcantara

Scepter

This 2023 edition of *Treatise on Prayer and Meditation* is based on the English translation of the original edition from 1556 which was translated into English in 1926 and edited by Dominic Chivas, O.F.M. and published in 1926 by Burns & Oates, London. The present work contains slight revisions to the translation for the sake of clarity for modern readers. Footnotes refer either to online or printed works in English or, if unavailable, to Spanish or Latin source texts.

Nihil obstat: Sylvester Nash, O.F.M. *Censor deputatus.*
Imprimi potest: Herbert Doyle, O.F.M. *Minister Angliae.*
January 23, 1926

Nihil obstat: G. H. Joyce, S.I. *Censor deputatus.*
Imprimatur: Edm. Can. Surmont, *Vicarius generalis.*
Westminster, April 29, 1926

This book is published in the U.K. by Scepter (U.K.) Ltd., 21 Hinton Ave., Hounslow, London TW4 6AP scepter@pobox.com and in the US by:

Scepter Publishers, Inc.
info@scepterpublishers.org
www.scepterpublishers.org
800-322-8773
New York

Cover image from Alamy.com
Cover and page design by Rose Design

ISBN: 9781594174735 (pbk)
ISBN: 9781594174742 (eBook)

Printed in the United States of America

Treatise
on
Prayer and Meditation

compiled by the Father
Brother Peter of Alcantara
Friar Minor of the Order of St. Francis

DEDICATED TO

The Most Magnificent and Most Devout
Signor Rodrigo De Chaves
of Ciudad Rodrigo

Most magnificent and most devout Lord:

I should never have compiled this little treatise nor consented to its publication had you not often commanded me to write something on prayer, in short and compendious form, and clearly, so as to be of service to all. This cheap and slender volume will be accessible even to the poor who cannot buy more expensive books, and, being written clearly will profit the simple who are not rich in understanding. I have deemed it a matter of no slight merit, in these circumstances, to obey one who demanded of me something so holy and fitting, thinking, also, that the merit of a work, due to so saintly a demand, would be very real. I shall profit by it myself, unless, indeed, the very great affection and tenderness I bear you, and your spouse and companion, Doña Francisca, bound to you by the ties of charity and love in Christ Jesus—our whole Good—as by those of marriage, unless—I say—this affection does not take from me some part of my merit.

However, if it is true, as indeed it is, that Christians participate in the good works of their brethren without diminishing at all thereby the merit of the latter, well may I say that I participate in your devotion and in all your good works, that you are my children most dear to me in the Lord and that you look on me as your father. The poverty of my doctrine and the zeal of my devotion have never failed you when there was question of your holy desires and lofty enterprises. After having read many books on this subject, I have briefly drawn out and gathered up from them what seemed to me the most profitable.[1]

God grant it may thus bring help to all who seek it, because for such also is it meant. You yourselves will win from it the spiritual reward of your good intentions, and I, the fruit of your good will All to the honour and glory of Jesus Christ our whole Good, from whom all good proceeds.

---

1. The Lisbon edition shows the saint's express reference, *among other books*, to that on Prayer *recently compiled by the very reverend Father Provincial, Brother Louis of Granada of the Friars Preachers.* From this, he writes, he has picked out and gathered all that is necessary to know about prayer. Père Ubald d'Alençon thus summarizes his own conclusions on the the authenticity of the *Treatise on Prayer*: (1) The author is certainly St. Peter, but (2) he used the larger treatise of Louis of Granada, making a kind of résumé of it, and giving extracts; but he acknowledges his source, a thing quite rare in those days. (3) It was written about 1556, probably at La Lapa (Badajoz). (4) Louis of Granada augmented his original work in 1566. Later editions of St. Peter's *Treatise* omit reference to Louis of Granada's work, presumably because the latter had fallen foul of the Spanish Inquisition; as did also for a short time, this very treatise of St. Peter.

Contents

PART II

PART III

Translator's Introduction

THE AUTHOR

St. Peter was born in 1499 at Alcantara, a Spanish town near the border of Portugal. Pope Alexander VI was reigning in Rome, and King Henry VII in England. Spain itself was mostly subject to the wise rule of Ferdinand and Isabella, and Peter's father was governor of their town of Alcantara. As a boy Peter studied law for two years in the university of Salamanca. At sixteen, after some interior anguish, he joined the Franciscan Order and received the brown habit at the convent of Manjarez from Father Michael Roco. After his profession he was sent to Belvis, and later to Badajoz. Ordained a priest in 1524, in the following year he was named Guardian of the convent of Los Angeles at Robredillo. For thirteen years Peter then threw himself into all the labors of an apostolic life and in much preaching. In 1538 he was elected Provincial of his Province of St. Gabriel. His favorite residence at this period was the convent of St. Michael at Plasencia, and it was here he drew up special statutes for the good ordering of his Province. He knew the convent well; it was a novitiate house, and already he had trained novices there.

In 1541, his term of office ended, he withdrew into Portugal, with Father John of Aguila. Some years back, King

John III and his family had begged Peter to visit him, so widespread was the fame of his sanctity. But Peter instead chose to live in a lonely region among the mountains of Arabida, lending the powerful influence of his name and example to help establish there a *custody*[1] of austere, contemplative Franciscans.

In 1544 he returned to Spain, as Definitor of the Province of St. Gabriel, and devoted himself once more to an apostolic life, and, very specially, to the growth of the Third Order. In 1548, at the Chapter held at Alconchel, he successfully overcame efforts to choose him once again as Provincial, and, this done, he returned again to Portugal to consolidate his former *custody,* which was suffering somewhat from the death of its chief promoter, Father Martin of St. Mary. In this work he was helped by his friend St. Francis Borgia. After three years he came back to Spain; in 1553 he was at the General Chapter of Salamanca, looking like "the living image"—as men thought—of his great father St. Francis of Assisi. Peter seems to have withdrawn into complete retirement, and, at La Lapa near Badajoz, about 1556, wrote his *Tratado de la Oración y Meditación.*

At this period he was busy about his own monastic *reform.* In 1555 we find him in Rome to secure the requisite authority. In the following year Rodrigo de Chaves, to whom the *Tratado* is dedicated, offered him a foundation at Pedroso. Peter accepted it, and there built up his *ideal* convent, in the most demanding spirit of poverty. Not even the appeal of the retired Emperor, Charles V, coupled with that

1. A small group of friaries, ruled by a Custos.

of St. Francis Borgia, could summon him back to Portugal. The *reform* spread rapidly by the double process of absorbing old foundations, already existing, and establishing new ones. By the end of the century it was, I suppose, the dominant Franciscan influence in Spain.

It was in this final period of his life that Peter dealt with St. Teresa of Avila. She acknowledges often, and in most generous terms, all the help he gave her, both individually for her own spiritual guidance, and exteriorly in the great work of rebuilding the Carmelite order.

On October 18, 1562, St. Peter died at Arenas, on his knees, and simultaneously appeared to St. Teresa, telling her "he was going to rest." He was beatified in 1622 and canonized on April 28, 1669.

The Book

APART FROM SOME LETTERS, a short writing on St. Teresa and the Constitutions of his Reform, the *Tratado de la Oración y Meditación* (Treatise on Prayer and Meditation) is the sole work left us by this master of an apostolic and spiritual life.[1] Like a better known work, emanating likewise from sixteenth century Spain, the *Tratado* might well be styled *The Spiritual Exercises of St. Peter of Alcantara,* for it is less a book of meditations than a guide to the interior life. Like the *Exercises* of St. Ignatius it begins by suggesting thoughts on the end of man, on death and judgement, on heaven and hell, and then passes forward to considerations on the humanity of Jesus Christ and his Passion. Where St. Ignatius has his *Contemplation for obtaining Love,* St. Peter gives us his *Special Prayer for the Love of God,* a prayer which is uniquely the saint's own work, and found in none of the writings on which he was drawing. It forms the culminating point of the book, and is redolent of that true Franciscan spirit of *affective* prayer.

---

1. The exquisite little treatise *Pax Animae,* familiar to many in Canon Vaughan's edition, and attributed to St. Peter, is really the work of a contemporary Spanish Franciscan, Father John of Bonilla. See *Traité de la Paix de l'Ame* by P. Ubald d'Alenqon: d2 Gigord, Paris, 1912, and *Introduction, infra,* p. 169. [Consequently, it has been omitted from this edition—*The Publishers.*]

It is also interesting to note the saint's teaching on contemplation. Needless to say, he sees nothing extravagant in the ordinary person aiming at it; on the contrary, it is the normal term of meditation and *discursive* prayer, which is but the "ladder" leading to contemplation. Meditation is the striking of the flint to secure the spark. "In contemplation, however," writes St. Peter, "the light is already lit—i.e., the sentiment and desired *affection of* the will is already present, and one rests thereon, and enjoys it in silence, no longer with much reasoning and speculation of the intellect, but just, with undivided attention, gazing upon truth."[2] Clearly the saint refers to *active* contemplation—a form of prayer to which all may aspire with God's accompanying grace. Very different is *passive* contemplation, a special gift of God to certain chosen souls, and not infrequently accompanied by "visions, revelations, ecstasies and so forth," which no one should desire and "which may be very dangerous indeed to such as are not grounded in humility."[3]

Of the book's value, it will be enough to recall what such saints as Teresa of Avila and Francis de Sales have said. The former, in the thirtieth chapter of *the Autobiography*, speaks of St. Peter's work on prayer as being "in the hands of almost everyone. And it is not surprising that one who practiced it with so much purity, should have written on it so well and so profitably." St. Francis de Sales in a letter to the wife of President Nicholas Brulart, (1544–1624), the Lord Chancellor of France, says "Alcantara is very good for prayer."[4] St. John of

2. Part I, ch. 12, 8th Counsel.

3. Part II, ch. 5, 2nd Counsel.

4. *Letters to Persons in the World*, ed. Mackey p. 68.

Avila, the famous apostle of Andalusia, eloquently praises St. Peter, and the Spanish Carthusian of Miraflores, Don Antony of Molina, recommends his sister to use the saint's little treatise in her study of mental prayer. In his own book, *Ejercicios Espirituales,* (*Spiritual Exercises*) he quotes approvingly the saint's advice in the matter of spiritual consolations.[5]

5. *Ejercicios Espirituales,* p. 47: Barcelona, 1776.

The Translation

IT MAY BE SAID AT ONCE that this translation would never have been made if it had not been for the guidance of Father Michael Bihl, O.F.M., pointing out where reliable texts were to be found, and for the ready kindness of Father Ubald d'Alençon, O.S.F.C., in allowing me to make free use of his own excellent French translation of the *Tratado.*[1] Without this it would have been quite impossible for me to embark on this undertaking, and it has been my main source throughout. I also made use of the Spanish text published at Medina del Campo in 1587 and lately reproduced by Father Andrew de Ocerin-Jauregui, O.F.M.[2] To this Spanish text I have made continuous reference, and have been able, in consequence, to supply here and there a word, or even a few lines, which appear to have been overlooked in the French translation. The earliest surviving edition of the treatise of St. Peter is, apparently, one published at Lisbon by John Blavio about 1558.

Father Giles Willoughby, a member of the second English Franciscan province, produced the first English translation in the seventeenth century. A copy of this book, with a *Life of*

1. *Traité de l'Oraison et de la Méditation*: Paris, Librairie Saint-François, 1923.

2. *Tratado de la Oración y Meditación*: Madrid, Hijos de Gregorio del Amo, 1919.

St. Peter prefixed, is, or was, in the library of the Franciscan Fathers at Forest Gate, in East London, where I read it some years back. The *Catholic Encyclopedia,* in the reference lists following the article on *Prayer,* mentions *The Golden Treatise of St. Peter of Alcantara* as having appeared at Oxford in 1906, but I have never seen nor been able to secure a copy of this translation.

Dominic Devas
Chilworth, England
February, 1926

Part I

1

On the Fruit One May Draw from Prayer and Meditation

AS THIS SHORT TREATISE deals with prayer and meditation, it will be useful to point out in a few words the fruit one may gather from this holy exercise. Thus with a more joyous heart will men apply themselves to it.

One of the greatest obstacles which hinders one from attaining supreme happiness and good is the heart's evil inclination, and thus the difficulty and disinclination to do what is right. Were it not for this, it would be a very easy thing to run in the path of virtue and to attain the end for which he was created. Hence St. Paul says: *I delight in the law of God, in my inmost self: but I see in my members another law at war with the law of my mind, and making me captive to the law of sin.*[1] Herein, then, you see the universal cause of all our evil.

To remove this distaste and difficulty and to help us in this affair, one of the most effective instruments is devotion. Devotion, as St. Thomas Aquinas says,[2] is nothing else than

1. Rom 7:22, 23.

2. Thomas Aquinas, *Summa Theologiae,* IIa IIae, q. 82, a. 1.

a certain promptitude and facility in well-doing, which banishes all difficulty and lethargy from our soul and prompts us to undertake all that is good. It is a spiritual nourishment, a refreshment, a dew from heaven, a breath wafted to us from the Holy Spirit, a supernatural *affection.* It so regulates, strengthens and transforms the heart of man as to give him a new taste and keenness for spiritual things, and a new distaste and horror for sensual things. Everyday experience shows us that, on emerging from profound and devout prayer, a spiritual person renews in himself all his good resolutions: he receives favors and steels himself in well-doing; he desires to please and love a Lord who has shown himself so good and so gentle; he thinks of accomplishing fresh deeds, and of suffering and of shedding his blood for him. In the end, he rejuvenates and renews all the freshness of his soul.

If you ask me how to win this so strong and noble affection of devotion, the same holy doctor replies that it is by means of meditation and contemplation on divine things. This deep meditation and thought does, in fact, engender that affection and sentiment in the will, which we call devotion, and this incites and urges us on to well-doing. Hence this holy exercise is highly recommended by all the saints. It is in itself a single virtue, but it prepares us and moves us forward to all the other virtues, and gives a general impulse to them all. If you would be convinced of this, see how clearly it is explained in the following words:

"If you would endure with patience the adversities and miseries of this life, be a soul of prayer. If you would acquire strength and courage to vanquish the temptations of the enemy, be a soul of prayer. If you would crush your self-will with all its inclinations and desires, be a soul of prayer. If you would know the wiles of Satan and defend yourself against his snares, be a soul of prayer. If you would live with a joyful heart, and pass lightly along the road of penance and sacrifice, be a soul of prayer. If you would drive away vain thoughts and cares which worry the soul like flies, be a soul of prayer. If you would nourish the soul with the sap of devotion and have it always filled with good thoughts and desires, be a soul of prayer. If you would strengthen and establish your heart in the way of God, be a soul of prayer. Finally, if you would uproot from your soul all vices, and plant virtues in their place, be a soul of prayer, for it is here that a soul receives the unction and grace of the Holy Spirit, who teaches all things.

Even more, would you mount to the summit of contemplation, and enjoy the sweet embraces of the Spouse, exercise yourself in prayer, for it is the road that leads to contemplation and to the taste of what is heavenly. Do you see now how great is the strength and power of prayer? In proof of all that has been said—apart from the witness of the divine Scriptures—let that suffice for the moment, as sufficient proof, what we have heard and seen, what we see every day—viz., many simple persons who have achieved all we have enumerated above, and even greater, by the exercise of prayer."[3]

What treasure could one find richer or more full? Listen again to what another very religious and holy doctor says on this subject, speaking of the same virtue. "In prayer," he says,

---

3. *Meditationes Vitae Christi,* c. 73, a work no longer to be ascribed to St. Bonaventure, but rather to the Franciscan, *Joannes a Caulibus.* See *Opera Omnia S Bonaventurae,* t. x of the Quaracchi edition.

"the soul cleanses itself from sin, charity is nourished, faith is strengthened, hope made secure; the spirit rejoices, the soul grows tender, and the heart is purified, truth discovers itself, temptation is overcome, sadness takes to flight, the senses are renewed, failing virtue is made good, tepidity disappears, the rust of sin is rubbed away. In it are brought forth lively flashes of heavenly desires, and in these fires burns up the flame of divine love. Great are the excellences of prayer, great its privileges. The heavens open before it, and unveil their secrets there, and to it are the ears of God ever attentive."[4]

Let this suffice to give some idea of the fruit of this holy exercise.

---

4. St. Lawrence Giustiniani, *Lignum Vitae: De Oratione*, c1-2, pp. 6–7, play.google.com/books/reader?id=LIk7AAAAcAAj@pg=GBS.PA6ehl=en_SG.

2

On the Subject Matter of Meditation

As we just saw the immense value of prayer and meditation, let us turn to how we ought to meditate. As the purpose of this holy exercise is to establish in our hearts the love and the fear of God and fidelity to his commandments, so the most suitable subject matter for this exercise will be what is most adapted to this end.

It is, of course, true that all material things, and all that is spiritual and sacred, may serve this purpose; still, speaking generally, the mysteries of our faith—as contained in the Creed—are the most efficacious and effective. Here, we focus on the benefits of God: the last judgement, the pains of hell, and the glory of heaven, and these act strongly upon our heart and move it to the love and fear of God. It treats also of the Life and Passion of Christ, our Savior.

Here, then, are two groups of subjects, specially noted in the *Creed;* and it is mostly around these that we ponder in meditation, so that with good reason is it said that the *Creed* contains the matter most suitable for this holy exercise. This, however, must not be taken to mean that that each one cannot find elsewhere what moves his heart to the love and fear of God.

To introduce newcomers and beginners into this path, and to provide them with the sustenance which suits them, already prepared and considered beforehand, I shall here give two sets of meditations for each day of the week, one for the evening and one for the morning, drawn, for the most part, from the mysteries of our faith. As we feed the body, so do we likewise feed the soul, whose nourishment lies in meditation on and consideration of divine things. Of these meditations, one set is on the Sacred Passion and Resurrection of Christ, the remainder on the other mysteries mentioned above. He who cannot find the time to recollect himself twice every day, can, at least, devote one week to the first set of mysteries, and the second week to the other; or he may confine himself to those on the Life and Passion of Jesus Christ, as these are the more important. It is not wise at the beginning of this effort, to neglect the others, for they are very suitable for that period in which the fear of God is required most of all, and for contrition and hatred of sin.

FIRST SERIES OF MEDITATIONS FOR EVERY DAY OF THE WEEK

Monday: Sin and Self-knowledge

Today you may occupy yourself with the remembrance of sin, and with the knowledge of yourself. The one will show you all the evil there is in you; the other will convince you that you have nothing which is not from God. This is the way to win humility, the mother of all the virtues.

Think, in the first place, of the many sins of your past life, especially of those you committed when you knew less of God. If you consider well, you will find them to be *more numerous than the hairs of my head,*[1] and that you lived, in those days, like a pagan who knows not God. Go briefly through the ten commandments of God and the seven deadly sins, and you will find there is not one into which you have not often fallen by action, by word, or by thought.

In the second place, think of all God's benefits, and of the different periods of your past life, in what fashion you have used them; for this must you render an account to God. Tell me: how have you spent your childhood, and your adolescence, and your youth, and in the end, the days of your past life? How have you used the senses of the body and the powers of the soul, which God has given you that you might know and serve him? How have you used your eyes, if not to gaze upon vanity? And your ears, if not to listen to falsehood? And your tongue, if not in every type of oath and slander? And your taste and smell and touch, if not in pleasures and sensual caresses?

How have you profited by the holy sacraments, which God has instituted for a remedy? How have you thanked him for his benefits? How have you corresponded with his inspirations? How have you used your health and energy, your natural talents, your material resources, the facilities and opportunities you have had of leading a good life? What interest have you had in your neighbor, whom God has commended to you, and in those works of mercy he has bidden you to engage in for his sake? What answer will you give on the day of reckoning, when God will say to you: *Turn in the*

1. Ps 40 (39):12.

account of your stewardship, for you can no longer be steward.[2] O barren tree, all prepared for eternal torments! How will you answer on that day when you must explain all your life, and every moment and minute thereof?

In the third place, think of the sins you have committed and commit every day since the time you opened your eyes to the knowledge of God. You will find that the old Adam,[3] *the sinful body,* still lives in you in many an old and deep-rooted habit. See how insolent you have been towards God, how ungrateful for his benefits, how rebellious to his inspirations, how slothful in his service. Never do you do anything for him with promptitude and diligence, nor with the requisite purity of intention, but other motives and worldly interests move you.

Consider, moreover, how hard you are towards your neighbor, and how compassionate towards yourself, a lover of your own will, of the flesh, of your honor and of your own interests. See how proud you are, and ambitious, hot-tempered, overbearing, vain and envious, full of malice, self-indulgent, inconstant, lacking respect, sensual, intent on your own amusements and conversations, your laughter and idle words. Mark your inconstancy in your good resolutions, how inconsiderate in your words, how negligent in your work, how weak and pusillanimous in every grave affair.

In the fourth place, having considered the great number of your sins, ponder on their seriousness that you may gauge every aspect of your wretchedness. To this end you ought

---

2. Lk 16:2.

3. Rom 6:6.

first to consider these three circumstances of the sins of your past life, namely: *Against whom* you have sinned; *Why* you have sinned; and *In what way* you have sinned.

If you look *against* whom you have sinned, you will see that you have sinned against God, whose kindness and majesty are infinite, whose benefits to man and whose mercies are more numerous than the sands of the sea. And *why* have you sinned? For a point of honor, for some bestial pleasure, for some tiny interest, and often for none at all, but just from custom and depreciation of God. *In what manner* have you sinned? With such ease, such boldness, so unscrupulously, so fearlessly, even, at times, with such readiness and content as if you were sinning against a God of wood, knowing and seeing nothing of what passes in the world. Is this the honor due to so great a majesty? Is this the gratitude for such great benefits? Is this the price of that precious blood, shed on the Cross, of those blows and buffets, received for you? Wretched in what you have lost, you are still more so in what you have done, and most of all, if you do not recognize your sorry plight.

After this it will be very useful to fix the eyes of your mind on the study of your own nothingness. Of yourself, you hold nothing at all except sin; all the rest comes from God. It is clear that the gifts of nature, and those of grace—which are the greater—are wholly his; to him belongs the grace of predestination (which is the source of all the other graces), to him the grace of vocation, to him concomitant (cooperating) grace, to him the grace of perseverance, to him the grace of eternal life. What have you then in which to glory but your nothingness and sin? Rest a little in the consideration of this nothingness—for this is all you have, the remainder is all God's—that you may see plainly and distinctly what you are and what he is, your poverty and his riches, and how little, in consequence, you should trust and esteem yourself, and how much you should trust in him, love him, and glorify yourself in him.

Thinking over all these points, have the very lowest possible esteem of yourself. Consider yourself as nothing better than a wild reed which bends before every wind, without weight or strength or firmness, unstable and with no sort of solidity. Consider yourself as Lazarus, four days in the tomb, a corpse tainted and horrible, full of worms, so that every passerby holds his nose and closes his eyes before such a sight. Imagine that you thus appear to God and his angels, hold yourself unworthy to lift your eyes towards heaven, unworthy of the earth that bears you, of the creatures that serve you, of the very bread you eat and the air you breathe. Cast yourself at the Savior's feet with her who was a public sinner,[4] cover yourself with the shame of a woman who has betrayed her husband. With great sorrow and repentance of heart ask forgiveness for your wanderings, that in his infinite goodness and mercy, he may deign to receive you back into his house.

Tuesday: On the Miseries of this Life

Today you will meditate upon the miseries of human life. Thus you will see how vain is the glory of the world, how fit

---

4. Lk 7.

to be despised, for it has no other frail foundation than this miserable life. The defects and miseries of this life are, as it were, innumerable. Consider especially the following seven:

First, that this life is short, some seventy or eighty years at most, and, if it stretches beyond, is, as the Psalm says, *their span is but toil and trouble.*[5] Take from this the period of infancy, which is more an animal than a human life, and the time spent in sleep, during which we neither use our senses nor that reason of ours which is proper to man, and you will see that life is even shorter than at first appears. If, moreover, you compare it with the eternity of the life to come, it will seem to you hardly a speck. Thus you will perceive how infatuated are those who, to enjoy so short a breath of life, risk the loss of the repose of what is to last forever.

Second, consider how uncertain is this life. Here is another misery to add to the former. As if its shortness were not enough, it is insecure and uncertain. How many reach those seventy or eighty years? For how many the strands are broken when they would begin to weave! How many pass away in the flower of their age—as we put it—or before they reach maturity! You *do not know*, as the Savior says, *when the master of the house will come.*[6] To appreciate this truth better, think of the deaths of the many persons you have known in this world, especially of your friends and comrades, and of persons who have been famous and admired. At varying ages in life has death struck them and swept away all their schemes and hopes.

5. Ps 90 (89):10.

6. Mk 13:35.

Third, consider how frail and delicate is this life, and you will see how no vessel of glass is as fragile. A breeze, or a hot sun, a draught of cold water, or the germs of a sick person are enough to despoil us of this life, as everyday experience shows. How many are cut down in the prime of life from one or other of these causes.

Fourth, see how changeable is this life, never the same for long. Our bodies do not remain permanently in one regular state of health; much less our souls. Like the sea they are always restless under the varying winds and waves of passion, of craving, of desire, which trouble us at every hour. Think, finally, of the changes of fortune: no one willingly consents to remain in the same state of life, with the same measure of prosperity, the same joy, but human life is like a wheel, for ever rolling on. Above all, dwell on the unceasing movement of life: day or night, it never pauses, lessening as it moves. What is our life but a torch which is forever consuming itself? The more resplendently it burns, the more rapidly will it flicker out. *He comes forth like a flower, and withers.*[7] It is by reason of this continuous change that God says, by the mouth of Isaiah, All *flesh is grass, and all its beauty is like the flower of the field.*[8] St. Jerome comments thus upon these words: "Truly, when we consider the frailty of our flesh, and how at every point and moment of time we increase and decrease, without ever remaining in the same state, and how what at this very instant forms the subject of our discourse, of our schemes and meditations, is so much cut off from our life, we shall not hesitate to speak of our flesh

7. Job 14:2.

8. Is 40:6.

as a little grass, and all its glory as the flower of the field."[9] The infant at the breast, how quickly it grows into a child, and the child into a big lad, and lo and behold, the big lad is soon well on in years, and, when on the verge of old age, marvels to find himself no longer young! The woman, whose beauty attracted the attention of so many young men, soon finds herself with wrinkled brow, and she who was once so attractive quickly becomes an object of aversion.

Fifth, consider how deceitful is life. This is perhaps the worst feature of all, so many does she lead astray, so many cling to her in blind affection. She is ugly, and we fancy her beautiful; bitter, and she appears to us sweet; short, and each one esteems her enduring; she seems spacious, and is narrow; she seems so lovable that there is no peril nor labor men will not face for her, even at the risk of life eternal, doing such things as lead them to the loss of the life which knows no end.

Sixthly, consider how this life, already burdened with those miseries we have mentioned, falls victim to so many misfortunes both of soul and body. Nothing else is it than a valley of tears and sea of measureless sorrow. St. Jerome relates how Xerxes, that mighty monarch, who levelled out the mountains and filled in the seas, found himself one day looking down from a height upon a countless host of armed men. He admired them for some time and then began to weep. Questioned on the cause of his tears, he replied: 'I weep because a hundred years hence not one of those I see before me will be alive.' "Would that we," adds St. Jerome, "could mount to some such height from where we might

9. St. Jerome, *Commentary on Isaias, chapter 40.*

view all the world at our feet. Then we might see the falls and disasters of all the world, nations destroyed one by the other, and kingdom by kingdom. Here we would see torments, and in another place massacre; some perishing at sea, others led away captive; here a wedding, there a death; some dying by violence, others in peace; some abounding in wealth, others begging. Finally, we should see not merely the army of Xerxes (antiquity) but all men in the world, living today, and doomed, in a few days, to vanish."[10]

Think of all the infirmities and labors of man's body, all the afflictions and anxieties of his soul, all the perils that accompany man in every state and in every period of his life, and you will see well enough the miseries of human life, and, clearly too, how little the world can give. Thus you will easily come to hold in little esteem all that there is in it.

To all these miseries succeeds the last, which is death. For body and soul alike this is the final terror. In an instant the body is stripped of all, and the soul fixed for ever in its eternity.

This meditation will help to make you understand how short and wretched is the glory of the world—yet it is on this that a worldly life relies—and in consequence how reasonable it is to disdain and scorn it.

Wednesday: On Death

Today you will think of that passing away which we call death. This is one of the most useful considerations for acquiring true wisdom and for avoiding sin, as well as for leading us to prepare in time for the hour of judgement.

---

10. St. Jerome, *Funeral Oration on Nepotian.*

Consider in the first place how uncertain is the moment in which death will lay you low. You know neither the day, nor the place, nor in what state you will be, when it comes. You know only that you must die, all the rest is uncertain; except this, that ordinarily it comes when a man is least desirous of it, and thinking least about it.

Secondly, consider the parting it occasions, not merely from the things we have loved in this life, but even between soul and body, so long such close partners. To be banished from one's country, and no longer able to breathe one's native air, is looked on as a great evil, though the exile carry with him all he loves: how much harder, then, will that exile be, which is total, withdrawing us from all that is in our house, from our possessions, from our friends, from our father and mother and sons, from air and light, and indeed from all things! The bull lows when separated from its mate with which it worked. What will be the cry of your heart when you are separated from the company of all those who help you in bearing the burdened yoke of life?

Consider, again, the distress a man experiences when he calls to mind the fate which awaits his soul and his body after death. For his body, he knows nothing better is in store than a sevenfoot grave, side by side with the other dead. For the soul, nothing sure, neither as to its future nor as to its fate. Here lies an anguish greater than which one cannot suffer. We know of glory and of unending pain, we are on the brink of the one or the other, yet are ignorant as to which of these two so unequal destinies awaits us.[11]

11. Eccles 9:1, 2.

To this yet another and no less an anguish succeeds: the account that we must render; even the most valiant tremble before this. The Desert Father, St. Arsenius, on the point of death began to tremble. "Father," said his disciples, "are you afraid now?" "My children," he answered, "This is no new fear which is upon me. It is one I have known and felt during my whole life."[12] At this moment, in fact, a man pictures all his sins as a squadron of hostile cavalry charging down upon him, and the greater sins—those in which he revelled the deeper—stand out conspicuous above the rest, and terrify him the more. Oh, how bitter now is the memory of those past delights which, at the time, seemed so sweet! Well does the wise man say: *Do not look at wine when it is red . . . At the last it bites like a serpent, and stings like an adder.*[13] These are the poisoned dregs of the drink the enemy proffers us, this is the bitter aftertaste from the gilded chalice of Babylon.

Surrounded by so many accusers, a man, thus wretched, begins to fear the terror of this judgement. "Miserable that I am," he says within himself, "to have lived in error, and walked by such paths as these: what will become of me in this judgement?" St. Paul tells us that *what things a man shall sow, those also shall he reap*:[14] and what have I sown, if not the works of the flesh; what can I look for, then, but corruption? St. John says that in the heavenly city all is pure gold, and that

12. Rufinus, *Life of St. Arsenius*, Book 3. Also from Louis of Granada, www.saintsquotes.net/selection.

13. Prov 23:31–32.

14. Gal 6:8.

nothing defiled shall enter in;[15] what, then, can he hope for who has lived a life so evil and so shameful?

Now come the sacraments of Confession and Communion, and of the Anointing of the Sick, the last comforts which the Church brings to us to help us in these terrible moments. See here again the anxiety and anguish suffered by the man who has led an evil life, how he wishes, now, that he had followed another course, how different a life would he lead henceforward, were time allowed him. He will indeed appeal to God, yet the pain and grip of disease will but hardly allow such recourse.

Note also the final accompaniments of the malady which herald the approach of death, how terrible they are and awe-inspiring: the heaving chest, the hoarse voice. The feet lose all sense of touch, the knees grow icy cold, the nose runs, the eyes sink in, the face is deathly white, the tongue can function no longer, and finally the soul battles to depart and all the tormented senses lose their power and strength. But above all it is the soul that suffers most; in agony she struggles, fearing to go, dreading the judgement that is being prepared. She has no natural desire for this separation, she clings lovingly to her state, she fears the tribunal of justice.

At length the soul leaves the body; and now two courses are open to you: by one you may accompany the body to the tomb; by the other, follow the soul and witness the final fixing of its fate. Consider what happens in both cases. Think of the body after the soul has left it. Rich apparel is produced in which to clothe it for burial, and then all possible speed is

15. Rev 21:21, 27.

made to remove it from the house. Consider all the details of the burial, the tolling bells, the questions men ask each other about the dead, the service in the church with its mournful music, the funeral procession and the weeping friends; in fact, all the circumstances that usually accompany the laying of a body in the tomb, the land of perpetual oblivion.

This done, turn to the soul and watch the road she takes towards these unknown regions, the place where she ultimately halts and the judgement that follows. Imagine yourself present at this judgement, and that the whole court of heaven is waiting there to hear the final sentence. Question will be asked and answer given for everything that you have received down to the very point of a needle. There must account be rendered for the gift of life and worldly goods, and family, for the inspirations of God and for all that might have helped you on to a holy life, and, above all, for the blood of Christ; and according to the account each one will render, so will he be judged.

Thursday: The Last Judgement

Today you will think of the last judgement. This consideration will foster in your soul those two important sentiments which should animate every faithful Christian: viz., fear of God, and hatred of sin.

Consider, in the first place, how terrible that day will be on which will be tried the case of every child of Adam, on which our own cases will be settled and the final sentence, as to our future, published. That day will gather to itself the days of every century, past, present and to come. Then the world shall render account of its ages, then the anger of God, pent up throughout the centuries, shall break forth. How impetuously this river of divine indignation will burst out, receiving as many affluent streams of wrath and anger as there have been sins committed from the beginning of the world.

Second, mark the dreadful signs heralding that day. Before that day comes, as the Savior says, And *there will be signs in sun and moon and stars,*[16] and, *in fine,* among all creatures in heaven and on earth. Before it is yet upon them, all will feel the end approaching, and in great distress will begin to tremble before they fall. Men will be *fainting with fear,* as they listen to the dreadful roaring of the sea, and watch the great waves and the raging tempest, terrible indications portending the awful calamities and miseries predicted for the world. They will wander about, stupefied and amazed, pallid and haggard, as men dead before death has reached them, as men judged before the sentence has been proclaimed, measuring their peril by their own fears, each one so busy over himself as to be heedless of his neighbor, even the father heedless of his child. None can serve his fellow, and yet none can stand alone.

Third, contemplate that universal deluge of fire which is to precede the coming of the judge; hearken to the challenging notes of the archangel's trumpet, summoning to one place all the generations of the world to be present at the judgement; see the awe-inspiring majesty of the approaching judge.

Fourth, turn now to the thought of the rigid severity of the account each one must render. Truly, as Job says, *How can a man be just before God. If one wished to contend with him,*

---

16. Lk 21:25, 26.

one could not answer him once in a thousand times.[17] What will the wicked feel when God examines each one, saying to him in the interior of his conscience: Come hither, you evil man, what have you seen in me to despise me thus, and to pass into the camp of my enemy? To my own image and likeness I have created you; I have given you the light of faith; I have made a Christian of you; with my own blood I have ransomed you. It was for you I fasted and journeyed, watched and toiled; for you my sweat became as drops of blood, for you I suffered persecution and blows, blasphemy and derision, mockery, dishonor, torments and at last the cross. See here the cross and the nails, see still upon my body the wounds of feet and hands, before this sky and earth I suffered and they bear witness still. What have you done with that soul of yours which I, by my blood, made mine? At what work have you employed what I so dearly won? O foolish and adulterous generation! Why have you rather sought in weariness to serve your enemy, than in joy to serve me, your Redeemer and Creator? So often I have called you, and you did not answer; I have knocked upon your door and you did not rouse yourself; I have stretched out my hands upon the cross, and you did not regard; you have despised my counsels, and all my promises and threats. It is for you now, angels of mine, to speak. Judge, judges, between me and my vine. *What more was there to do for my vineyard, that I have not done in it?*"[18]

What reply shall the wicked give, those who have made a mockery of divine things, who have ridiculed holiness,

---

17. Job 9:2, 3.

18. Is 5:4.

who have despised simplicity, who have preferred the laws of the world to those of God: men deaf to every voice of God, insensible to every inspiration, rebellious against his commandments, hard and ungrateful before chastisements and benefits alike? How shall they make answer who have lived as though they had no belief in God, and knew no other law than that of their own interest? What *will you do*, says Isaiah, *on the day of punishment, in the storm which will come from afar?*[19] From whom will you seek help, and of what value to you now will be the abundance of your wealth?

And now, fifth, consider the terrible sentence which the Judge will deliver upon the wicked, and the awful words which long will linger in the ears of all who hear them. His lips *are filled with indignation, and his tongue is like a devouring fire.*[20] What fire will leap to flame like these words *Depart from me, you cursed, into the eternal fire prepared for the devil and his angels?*[21] What depth of thought and meaning beneath each single word! Separation, malediction, fire, the company, and, above all, the eternity.

Friday: The Pains of Hell

Today you will meditate upon the pains of hell. This meditation will confirm your soul more, both in the fear of God and in horror of sin.

These pains, St. Bonaventure tells us, should be considered under those material aspects and figures such as the

19. Is 10:3.

20. Is 30:27.

21. Mt 25:41.

saints have taught us. Thus it is well, he tells us, to imagine the place of hell as a subterranean lake dark and obscure, or as a very deep well full of flames, or as a black and terrible city consumed by raging fires, reechoing to the cries and groans of tormentors and tormented alike, with endless weeping and gnashing of teeth.

This dreadful abode gives rise to two principal kinds of pain: what is called the pain of *sense,* and also the pain of *loss.* As for the former, reflect how there is no exterior nor interior sense that will not have its own proper pain. The wicked have indeed offended God with all their members and all their senses, and have made of everything an instrument of sin.

Thus it will be ordained that each suffer its proper torment and pay its debt. Here the eyes of adultery and evil living shall endure the awful vision of devils. There the ears that have hearkened to lying and obscenity will listen to unending blasphemy and groans. Here the sense of smell, which has revelled in the scents of sensual odors of vice, will be filled with an intolerable stench. There the taste, which has regaled itself in gluttony and varied dishes, will be tormented with a devouring hunger and thirst. Here the tongue, which has been addicted to murmuring and blasphemy, shall feel a bitterness as of the venom of dragons. There the touch, which has lingered lovingly in sweet, caressing blandishments, will wade as Job says [22] amid the icy waters of the river of lamentation, Cocytus.

Here the imagination will be racked by the apprehension of the present sufferings, the memory by the recollection of past pleasures, the understanding by the thought of future

22. Job 24:19.

ills, and the will by the immensity of anger and rage which the wicked will entertain against God.

There, finally, will be gathered up in one all the evils and torments imaginable. "There will be a cold past all endurance," says St. Gregory, "an unquenchable fire, the worm that does not die, an intolerable odor, darkness that is palpable, the fierce blows of the tormentors, the sight of devils, the disorder of sin, and the despair at seeing the loss of all that is good."[23]

Tell me now, if it is already so insupportably hard to endure even the least of these evils, and for the very shortest space of time, what will it be to suffer at one and the same moment, and in all one's members, and senses both interior and exterior, all this multitude of evils, and that, not for the space of one night or a thousand, but throughout an infinite eternity? By what sense or words or judgement can we in this world grasp or fathom this reality?

However, this is not the greatest of the pains endured. Greater, beyond all comparison, is what theologians call the *pain of loss.* This consists in being forever deprived of the vision of God, and of his glorious presence. Now, just as any pain is the greater in proportion to the greatness of the good of which it deprives a man, so, as God is the greatest good of all, the loss of him will be the greatest evil that there can possibly be.

Such are the pains which, in general, all of the damned suffer; but, besides these general torments, each suffers particular ones according to the nature of his sin. There will be

---

23. Pope St. Gregory, *Moralia,* book 9, chapter 46.

a special torment for the proud, for the envious, for the avaricious, for the impure, and so on for the rest. The pain will be commensurate with the sin committed, the shame with the proud presumption of the past, the nakedness with the superabounding excess, the hunger and thirst with the gluttonous pleasures of other days.

With all these torments is coupled that *eternity of suffering* which is as the seal and lock upon them all. Everything, in fact, may be endured which has an end; for nothing that is transient is really great; but a pain that is endless, without alleviation, decline or diminution, without any prospect of ever ceasing to continue, neither the torment itself, nor the one who inflicts it, nor he who suffers it, a veritable banishment, a clinging garment which may never be laid aside, this indeed breaks the spirit of anyone who attentively considers it.

This is, in fact, the greatest of all the sufferings endured. For if some limit might be set to the endurance of these afflictions a thousand years, or a hundred thousand years—or if, as Pope St. Gregory puts it, "they hoped to see the end, after having drunk all the waters of the ocean by taking a single drop once every thousand years, this would be to them a source of unending consolation."[24] But it is not so: these pains will last with the eternity of God. The duration of these miseries will be measured by that of the divine glory. As long as God shall live, so long shall death endure. When God ceases to be what he is, then the damned shall cease to be what they are.

24. Pope St. Gregory, *Moralia*, book 9, chapter 9.

Upon this unending eternity of duration, I beg you, dear brother of mine, cast your eyes, and reflect. Ponder within yourself, quite frankly, upon these truths. In his Gospel the Eternal Truth speaks to us: *Heaven and earth will pass away, but my words will not pass away.*[25]

Saturday: On Heaven

Today you will consider the glory of the blessed, that, thus, your heart may be moved to the contempt of the world, and to a desire of their company. That you may gather some idea of their felicity think of these five features of heaven, namely, its excellence, the happiness of those who are there, the vision of God, the glory of the body, and finally the complete gathering together there of every good thing.

First, see the excellence of the place, and particularly its magnificent spaciousness. We have seen, in competent authors, that each one of the stars is greater than the earth; some, indeed, so immense as to be ninety times larger. Looking up into the heavens we see there a veritable multitude of stars thrown across the empty spaces, from where a whole infinity of things might come down to us. How shall we not stand astonished and abashed at seeing the immensity of heaven and, what is greater still, that of the Sovereign Lord who made it?

As for its beauty, no words can express it. In this valley of tears, in this place of exile, God has created objects admirable and of great beauty. What has he not fashioned then in that

25. Mt 24:35.

place where his glory dwells, the throne of his greatness, the palace of his Majesty, the home of his thoughts and the paradise of all his delights?

After the excellence of the place, consider the nobleness of its inhabitants, their number, their sanctity, their riches and their unimaginable beauty. St. John says that the multitude of the elect is so great that no one may count them.[26] St. Dionysius the Areopagite says that the number of the angels is so great that it surpasses, beyond compare, that of all material things on the earth.[27] St. Thomas, following this opinion, teaches that the extent of heaven is greater, beyond all proportion, than that of the earth, and that the multitude of heavenly spirits similarly exceeds that of all material things in the world.[28]

What more admirable can one conceive? Well weighed, this of itself should suffice to astonish all men.

Moreover, each one of these blessed spirits—even the least among them—is more beautiful than all this visible world. What will it be, then, to see such numbers of magnificent beings like this, to gaze upon the perfections and offices of each one of them? The angels are the messengers of God; the archangels, ministering spirits; the powers, triumphal leaders; the virtues are all resplendent in glory; the thrones blaze out in light; the Cherubim shine in brilliance and the Seraphim are all aglow; and all sing together the canticles of God. If the mere presence and interchange of all this good

---

26. Rev 5:11.

27. St. Dionysius, *De Coelesti Hierarchia,* chapter 14.

28. St. Thomas Aquinas, *Summa Theologiae,* Part Ia, q50, article 3.

have such charm and sweetness, what will it be to be present there amongst so many happy ones, to speak with the apostles, converse with the prophets, and have communion with the martyrs and all the elect?

Where there is so much glory in rejoicing in the company of the good, what will there be in rejoicing in the company and in the presence of him whom the stars of the morning praise, whose beauty sun and moon admire, before whose ineffable qualities the angels and all the heavenly spirits fall prostrate? What will it be to behold this all-comprehensive Good, in whom all that is good in the world resides; even more, in whom is every world; who, though *One,* yet carries all things; though *Simple,* yet includes within himself all perfections? If it was so wonderful a thing to see and hear Solomon the King, so that the Queen of Sheba exclaimed, *Happy are these your servants, who continually stand before you and hear your wisdom.*[29] what will it be to behold this supreme Solomon, this eternal wisdom, this infinite greatness, this inestimable beauty, this immense goodness, and to rejoice therein for ever? Here, then, is the essential glory of the saints, our last end and the harbor of all our desires.

Pass on now to consider the nature of the glorified body. Each will enjoy four special qualities: *subtlety, agility, impassibility* and *clarity,* and the last named will be so great that the righteous will shine like the sun in the kingdom of their Father.[30] If a single sun, set in the midst of the heavens, suffices to give light and joy to all this world, what will be

29. 1 Kings 10:8.

30. Mt 13:43.

the effect of so many suns, of so many resplendent bearers of light?

And now, what can one say of all the other blessings of heaven? There, will be health, and no sickness; liberty, and no servitude; beauty, and no unsightliness; immortality, and no decay; abundance, and no want; repose, and no cares; security, and no dread; knowledge, and no error; satiety, and no feelings of revulsion; joy, and no sorrow; honour, and no contention.

There, says St. Augustine, *will true glory be, and where no one will be praised by mistake or flattery; true honor will not be refused to the worthy; likewise, no one unworthy will pretend to be worthy, where only those who are worthy will be admitted. There true peace will reign where no one will experience opposition either from self or others. God himself will be virtue's reward. He gives virtue and has promised to give himself as the best and greatest reward that could exist.*[31] One will see him for ever, love him for ever without wearying, and praise him, without fatigue. There, a resting place, spacious, beautiful, resplendent and sure; a companionship sweet and agreeable, an even tenor of time without evening or morning, but continuous in an indivisible eternity.

It will be as a perpetual summer there, freshened with the undying breath of the Holy Spirit. All are full of joy, all hymn and praise this sovereign Benefactor, through whose bounty they live and reign eternally. O heavenly city, secure abode, land of delight: O happy citizens, without any grief, tranquilly dwelling there, true men, but now at last

31. St. Augustine, *The City of God,* chapter 22, 30. Quoted in the *Catechism of the Catholic Church,* #2550.

unburdened. Ah, would that my combat were ended, the days of my exile done! When shall I go and stand before the face of my God?"[32]

Sunday: The Benefits of God

Consider, today, the benefits of God. Render thanks for them to the Lord, and enkindle in yourself a deeper love of One who is so good to you. These benefits are innumerable, but you may at least consider the five principal ones—viz., creation, conservation, redemption, vocation, and finally, all personal and hidden favors.

First, the benefit of *creation:* Consider very attentively what you were before being created, what God has done for you, what he has given you, prior to any merit on your part—namely, this body with all its members and senses, this soul so excellent, with its three notable faculties, the understanding, the memory and the will. Note well that in giving you this soul, all else is given you; for there is no perfection at all in any creature which man, in his own measure, does not possess. To give us, then, this single gift was, at the same time, to bestow everything else on us as well.

As for the benefit of *conservation*, see how utterly your whole being depends upon the providence of God. Not one instant would you live, not one step would you move were it not for him. Everything in the world he has created for your service: sea and land, birds and fishes and animals, the plants and even the very angels in heaven. See how he has given you

---

32. St. Augustine, *The City of God*, 1, 22, c. 30.

health and strength, life and nourishment, and all other temporal succor. Above all, think seriously of the miseries and disasters befalling other men daily, into which you also might easily fall if God, in his bounty, did not preserve you.

As for the benefit of *redemption,* consider these two points: firstly, the number and grandeur of the benefits he has given us by the grace of redemption, and, secondly, the number and greatness of the woes he suffered in his body and in his most holy soul in order to secure these blessings. To appreciate better what you owe to the Lord for all that he has suffered for you, consider these four principal points in the mystery of his Sacred Passion—namely, who it is that suffers; what he suffers; for whom, and why he suffers.

Who suffers? God. What does he suffer? The greatest torments and dishonor that anyone has ever endured. For whom does he suffer? For creatures, depraved, abominable and, by their actions, like to the very devils themselves. Why does he suffer? Not for his own advantage, nor for any merit in us, but on account of the depth of his own infinite love and mercy.

As for the benefit of *vocation,* consider in the first place how great was the bounty of God in making you a Christian, in calling you, through baptism, to the faith, and allowing you to participate in the other sacraments. And if, despite this call, you have lost your innocence, it is he who has drawn you out from sin, reestablished you in grace and set you anew on the path of salvation. How can you praise him enough for this kindness? How great has been his mercy in thus guarding you so long, in putting up with so many sins, in giving you so many inspirations, instead of cutting short the thread of life, as he does for others in the same state. How mighty has been his grace in raising you from death to life, and in opening your eyes to the light: and, after your conversion, how great has been his mercy in giving you the grace to sink to sin no more, to overcome the enemy and to persevere in good.

So much for the benefits open and recognized. Besides these, are others, secret ones, known only to him who has received them, and some indeed so hidden that even the recipient does not know them, but only he who bestows them. How many times in this life, by your pride or negligence or ingratitude, have you not deserved that God should abandon you, as he would have done many others, and yet he has not done so. From how many sins and occasions of sin has not the Lord, in his providence, preserved you by destroying the nets of the enemy, breaking up the way, and bringing to nought his schemes and devices. How often has he not treated us as he did St. Peter, saying, *Behold, Satan demanded to have you that he might sift you like wheat, but I have prayed for you that your faith may not fail.*[33]

Who but God alone knows these secrets? God's positive benefits, man may at times recognize, but the negative ones, which consist not in bestowing favors upon us but in delivering us from evils, who shall recognize these? For these, as well as for the others, we should of right always render thanks to the Lord. We should recognize ourselves as insolvent; so much does the total of our debts surpass that of our means of repayment as to be beyond all reckoning.

---

33. Lk 22:31, 32.

3

The Fitting Time and Value of these Meditations

HERE, THEN, DEAR READER, are the first seven meditations, on which you may contemplate, and occupy your mind each day of the week. You may also consider other subjects, and set aside certain days on which to do so, for whatever subject leads our heart to the love and to the fear of God, and to the keeping of his commandments, is fitting matter for meditation. However, it was necessary to draw out these subjects a little, because, on the one hand, they embody the principal mysteries of our faith which, of their own nature, are calculated to lead us on to good, and, on the other, because beginners, who have need of milk,[1] will find here—all made ready and prepared for them—the subjects on which to meditate. You need not grope your way forward like pilgrims in a strange country, or to hesitate in your movements, taking up one subject, rejecting another, and so on, without ever fixing themselves on any.

Remember, also, that these meditations are very suitable at the beginning of one's conversion, when a person once

1. 1 Cor 3:2.

more returns to God. These subjects move us to contrition and to a horror of sin, to the fear of God and to contempt of the world, which are all first steps in the path of virtue: and beginners ought to spend more time in the consideration of these subjects in order to establish themselves in holiness and in the virtues named above.

4

Seven Meditations on the Sacred Passion, and the Method to Be Used

HERE, NOW, are the seven meditations on the holy Passion, Resurrection and Ascension of Christ, to which one may add more on the other principal circumstances of his most holy life.

Note that in the Passion of Christ, six points merit our consideration: the greatness of his sufferings, that we may raise our level of compassion; the gravity of our sin, which caused them, that we may detest it; the immensity of the benefit, that we may be grateful; the excellence of the divine bounty and love, which shine forth there, that we too may render love in return; the fittingness of the mystery, that we may admire it; the many virtues of Christ, resplendent here, that we may imitate them.

As we meditate we should incline our heart to compassion for Christ's sorrows, which were the greatest in the world on account of the delicateness of his body, the greatness of his love, and the fact that they were endured without any kind of consolation, as has been said elsewhere. Or, again, we may draw motives of sorrow for our own sins, seeing that they were the cause of the many and great sufferings he endured; or, again, we may find motives of love and gratitude, considering the immensity of the love which he shows us, and the grandeur of the gift he has given us in redeeming us so fully at such cost to himself and such profit for ourselves. Or, again, we may lift up our eyes and consider the fittingness of the means which God has chosen to heal our wretchedness, to satisfy our debts, to relieve our needs, to enable us to win his grace, to humble our pride, to lead us on to contempt for the world, to a love of the cross, of poverty, of austerity, of injuries, and of every other virtuous and fitting act.

Yet again we may turn our attention to the splendid examples of holiness he has left us in his most sacred life and death, his meekness and patience, his obedience and mercy, his poverty and penance, his charity, humility, kindness and modesty, and all the other virtues which shine forth in his actions and words more brilliantly than the stars of heaven. Let us imitate what we see in him that the spirit and grace we have received from him may not find us idle, and thus, through him, we shall come to him. Here is indeed the highest and most useful way of meditating on the Passion of Christ, the way, namely, of imitation, for such imitation gradually transforms us, so that we may come to say, with the Apostle, *It is no longer I who live, but Christ who lives in me.*[1]

It is fitting, moreover, in all these mysteries, to consider Christ as present before our eyes, and ourselves as there with him in his sufferings, and not merely to think of the history of the Passion as a whole, but all the circumstances of it, and

1. Gal 2:20.

especially the following four: *who* is suffering; *for whom* he suffers; *how* he suffers, and for *what reason.*

Who suffers? God, all-powerful, infinite, immense. *For whom* does he suffer? For the most ungrateful and thankless creature in the world. How does he suffer? With a very great humility and love, kindness and meekness, with mercy, patience and mildness. For *what reason* does he suffer? Not for any interest of his own, nor worthiness on our part, but on account of the depths of his infinite pity and mercy.

Finally, let no one content himself with considering the exterior sufferings of Christ, but rather and much more deeply should he ponder on the interior ones. We should fix our attention far more on the soul than on the body of Christ, in order to appreciate his sorrows, his intimate feelings, and his thoughts.

After this little introduction, let us begin to take up again and give in order the mysteries of his Sacred Passion.

SEVEN MEDITATIONS ON THE SACRED PASSION

Monday: The Washing of the Feet, and the Institution of the Blessed Sacrament

Today, after having made the sign of the Cross and the usual preparation, let us consider the washing of the feet and the institution of the Most Blessed Sacrament.

Consider, O my soul, in, this scene, the gentle and kind Jesus: see the wonderful example of humility he gives you in rising up from the table and washing the feet of his disciples. O good Jesus, what is this you are about? O gentle Jesus, why do you thus humiliate your majesty so deeply? My soul, what feelings would have been yours in seeing Jesus kneeling at the feet of these men, at the feet of Judas? How hard you are, that your heart is not moved when faced with such great humility! How is it that such great meekness does not rend your heart? Can it be that you have made up your mind to barter away this gentle Lamb? Is it possible that even with this example before you, you have still no feelings of compassion? White and beautiful hands, how can you touch these feet soiled and repulsive? Most pure hands, how comes it that you do not shrink with horror from washing these feet covered with the filth of the roads and stained with blood? O Blessed Apostles, do you not tremble before such a manifestation of humility? Peter, what are you about? Are you, by chance, going to allow the Lord of Majesty to wash your feet? Quite taken aback and astonished at seeing his Lord prostrate before him, St. Peter exclaims: *Lord, do you wash my feet!*[2] Are you not the Son of the Living God? Are you not the creator of the world, the beauty of heaven, the paradise of the angels, the saving hope of men, the splendor of the Father's glory, the source of the wisdom of God in highest heaven? And yet would you seek to wash my feet! You, the Lord of such great majesty and glory, do you wish to fulfil so lowly a task?

Consider also how, as he finished washing the feet, he wipes them with the holy towel with which he is girded. With the eyes of the soul you may see there an image of the Mystery of our Redemption. See how, with the linen cloth, he wipes away all the dirt from these soiled feet; they become

2. Jn 13:6.

clean, and the linen all stained and soiled with the work. What more sullied than man conceived in sin, and what purer and more beautiful than Christ conceived of the Holy Spirit? *My beloved is all radiant and ruddy,* says the Spouse, *distinguished among ten thousand.*[3] It is he, so beautiful and so pure, who wills to take upon himself the stains and filth of our souls; he leaves them clean and free from it all, but with it all he himself appears on the Cross shattered and disfigured.

Finally, consider the words with which the Saviour concludes this act: *For I have given you an example, that you also would do as I have done to you.*[4] Do not refer these words simply to what has taken place and to this example of humility, but also to all the actions of the life of Christ, for it is a very perfect mirror of all the virtues, and especially of what is, in this incident, unfolded before us.

OF THE INSTITUTION OF THE MOST BLESSED SACRAMENT

To understand something of this mystery, remember, to begin with, that no human language can express the magnitude of the love which Christ has for his spouse the Church, and which, in consequence, he has also for every soul in grace, seeing that each one such is also his spouse.

Thus it was that this very tender consort, when about to quit this life and leave his spouse, the Church, that his absence might not lead to forgetfulness, left as a memorial

---

3. Song 5:10.

4. Jn 13:15.

this most holy Sacrament, in which he himself resides, seeking no other thing than his own self with which to perpetuate this mutual remembrance. During so long an absence he wished to leave his spouse a companion that she might never find herself alone, and thus he left to her this Sacrament, in which he is himself; and no better companion could he have found for her. He wished also to suffer death for his spouse, and thus to redeem her, and to enrich her with the price of his blood. And that she might rejoice at will in this treasure, he has, in this Sacrament, left her the key, for, as St. John Chrysostom tells us, *when you approach that awful cup, you may so approach, as desiring for the very side of Christ.*[5]

Moreover, this heavenly consort desired to be loved by his spouse, in return, with a very great love. To this end he arranged this mystic food, consecrated by such words that he who worthily receives it is both touched and wounded with this love.

He wished also to reassure his spouse, to give her pledges of this blessed possession of glory, that, compassed by this hope, she might traverse joyfully the toiling bitterness of life: and that the spouse might hold as certain and assured this hope of blessedness, he left her this ineffable treasure as a pledge, equal in itself to all she hopes for. Thus she need never despair of God giving all to her in that state of glory and of spiritual existence, since he does not refuse it to her here in this valley of tears where she lives in the flesh.

---

5. St. John Chrysostom, *Homily 85 commentary on Jn 19:35,* Nicene and Post-Nicene Fathers, v14, Christian Literature Publishing Co, Buffalo NY, www.newadvent.org/fathers/2401.htm.

He willed also, at the hour of his death, to make a testament and leave to his spouse some resplendent gift; and so he left her the most precious thing he had, and the most useful for her, since, in this gift, he left God to her. And, finally, he wished to leave our souls a sufficient provision and nourishment on which to live, for the soul has no less need of special sustenance for her spiritual life than the body has for its physical life. Thus it has come about that this wise physician, who knows so well the fluctuations of our feebleness, has instituted this Sacrament, and set it in the form of nourishment. The very fashion of its institution shows us the effect which it accomplishes and the need which our souls have of it: similar indeed, to the need our bodies have of suitable nourishment.[6]

Tuesday: The Prayer in the Garden, the Arrest, and the Events before Annas

Today you will think of the prayer in the garden, the seizing of the Savior, and the entry into and the affronts endured in the house of Annas.

Consider, in the first place, how our Savior, after the mysteries of the Supper were concluded, went with his disciples into the garden of Olives to pray there before entering into the battle of his Passion. He did this to teach us how, in all the labors and temptations of this life, we should always have recourse to prayer as to a sacred anchor. By his virtue, either the whole weight of tribulation will be lifted from us,

6. *The Spiritual Exercises of St. Ignatius: Third Week, First Contemplation, Fourth Point.* www.sacred-texts.com/chr/seil/seil31.htm.

or—and this is a yet greater grace—strength will be given us to support it.

On the way he went in company with three disciples very dear to him: St. Peter, St. James and St. John. These had been the witnesses of his glorious Transfiguration, and now they were themselves to see how different from the radiance of that vision would be the form he was about to assume for love of men. That they might see how the interior sufferings of his soul were no less than those which began to manifest themselves outwardly, he uttered these sad words: *My soul is very sorrowful even to death: remain here, and watch with me.*[7]

After these words our Lord withdrew himself a stone's throw from his disciples, and prostrate on the ground, in an attitude of profound respect, he began his prayer, saying: *My Father, if it be possible, let this cup pass from me; nevertheless, not as I will, but as you will.*[8] This prayer he recited three times, and, at the third, he entered into such agony that he began to sweat drops of blood which flowed all over his sacred body and, threading their way down, dropped to the ground. Consider our Lord in this sorrowful state, and see how the vision of himself, in all the sufferings he is to endure, passes before his mind. He apprehends perfectly the very cruel torments which are being made ready for the most sensitive of human frames; he calls to mind all the sins of the world—the cause of his sufferings—and the ingratitude of so many souls who will fail to recognize this benefit and to profit by so great and costly a remedy.

7. Mt 26:38.

8. Mt 26:39.

His soul is thus so many ways straitened, his senses and most delicate frame so troubled, that the muscles and members of his body become distended and his sacred flesh opens on all sides and allows the blood to pass out in such abundance as to flow on to the ground. If the prospect of future suffering brings such anguish upon the body, what must be the state of the soul which directly comprehends it?

See now, when the prayer is finished, that false friend arrives with his hateful company. He has forsworn his function of apostle and become chief and captain of the army of Satan. Watch him as he steps out in front of all the others, and, drawing near to the good Master, barters him away with a feigned kiss of peace. Then our Lord says to those who have come to seize him: *Have you come out as against a robber with swords and clubs to capture me? Day after day I sat in the Temple teaching, and you did not seize me; but this is your hour and the power of darkness.*[9] How amazing a mystery is this! What more astonishing than to see the Son of God assume the figure not merely of a sinner but of a condemned criminal. "This," he says, "is your hour and the power of darkness." He shows that the moment had come in which the most innocent Lamb was to be delivered into the power of the princes of darkness—that is, of the demons—to be subjected, at the hands of their ministers, to every torment and cruelty imaginable. Think to what depths of abasement this highness divine has lowered himself for you, since he abandons himself to the last of all evils, being delivered into the hands of devils. This is the pain your sins have deserved; he chooses to suffer it that you may be in a position to deliver yourself from it.

9. Mt 26:55, Lk 22:53.

After these words the whole pack of these hungry wolves lay hold upon this gentle Lamb. Some clutch him on one side, some on another, each one as he may. How roughly they treat him: what insults they shower upon him; how they push and strike him; what cries and brawling, like that of hunters with their prey. They snatch those saintly hands which, but a short time before, had worked such miracles, they bind them strongly with running knots, but so awkwardly that the flesh of the arms is all torn, and the blood flows. Thus, covered with ignominy, they drag him through the public streets.

Contemplate him on this journey, separated from his disciples, surrounded by his enemies, hurried along at breakneck speed, breathing heavily, the features all strained, the face red and inflamed by the hurry of the march. And yet, in the midst of this iniquitous treatment of his person, note his pervading calm, the gravity of his eyes, and that aspect wholly divine which, in the midst of the world's scorn, could yet never be obscured.

Come with our Lord to the house of Annas: see how he answers courteously the question put him by the high priest about his disciples and his doctrine, and how one of those wicked bystanders gave him a great blow on the cheek, saying: *Is that how you answer the high priest? Jesus answered him, If I have spoken wrongly, bear witness to the wrong; but if I have spoken rightly, why do you strike me?*[10] Admire here, O my soul, not merely the mildness of this answer, but also that divine countenance, bruised and discolored by the force of the blow, the modesty of those serene eyes, that untroubled brow, and,

10. Jn 18:22, 23.

within, that most holy soul, so humble and so ready, should the aggressor demand it, to turn the other cheek.[11]

Wednesday: Before Caiaphas: The Denial of St. Peter and the Scourging

Today we think of our Lord brought before the high priest Caiaphas, of the torments of that night, of Peter's denial, and of the scourging at the pillar.

Consider first how our Lord is led from the house of Annas, which he entered first, to that of the high priest Caiaphas. Bear him company. See how the sun of justice is eclipsed, and this divine face, on which the angels desire to look,[12] is covered with spittle. The Savior, sworn in the name of God to say who he was, replied as was fitting; but these men, unworthy of so noble an answer, are blinded by the splendor of so clear a light. They turn upon him once more, like wild beasts, and pour forth their anger and their rage. They shower upon him punches and blows; with their vile mouths they spit upon this divine face; they blindfold him, strike and mock him, saying, *Prophesy: who is it that struck you.*[13] O wonderful humility and patience of the Son of God! O this face, beauty of the angels, was it made to be spat upon? Men are likely to turn to some sordid corner when they wish to spit. In all this great palace was there no

11. See *The Spiritual Exercises of St. Ignatius: Third Week, Second Contemplation.* www.sacred-texts.com/chr/seil/seil18.htm.

12. 1 Pet 1:12.

13. Lk 22:64.

viler place to sully than your countenance? Can you, who are mere earth and dust, refrain, with this example before you, from humbling yourself?

Turn, next, to consider the sufferings the Savior endured during this bitter night. The soldiers on guard mocked him, as St. Luke tells us, and to master their inclination for sleep they strike the Lord of Majesty and frolic with him. See, O my soul, how this most gentle Spouse serves as target for the arrows of all their blows and cuffs. O cruel night! Weighed down with misery! My good Jesus, there was no sleep for you, nor was there slumber for those tormenting you. Night was made that all creatures might find their rest in it, and that sense and limb, wearied with the day's work, might be renewed.

This is the moment those evil men chose to torment your senses and your limbs, by wounding your body, distressing your soul, binding your hands, buffeting your face, spitting upon your person, offending your ears, so that, at the time when all the members are likely to be at rest, in you all suffer and are in pain. How different are these morning chants from those the angels in heaven are at this moment singing to you. There they sing, *Holy, Holy*: and here, *Let him die, let him die; Crucify him, crucify him.* O angels in paradise, you hear this double stream of sound. What feelings are yours as you watch him being so maltreated on earth, towards whom you, in heaven, are showing so much reverence? What must your thoughts be as you watch God bearing these sufferings for the sake of the very same persons who are inflicting them? Who ever knew an act of love like this, to suffer death in order to deliver from death the very one who is causing it?

The torments of this sorrowful night grew greater still with Peter's denial. This intimate friend, chosen to witness the glory of the Transfiguration, honored, among all, with the headship of the Church: he is the first of all, not merely once, but three times, to swear and swear again, in the very presence of this same Lord, that he knew him not, knew not, even, who he was. O Peter, was he then so evil a man, there before you, that you should feel so much ashamed that you knew him? You are to be the first to condemn him, even before the high priests, since you let it be understood that it is a dishonour to know him. Could any deeper injury be done him than that? *And the Lord turned and looked at Peter.*[14] He cast his eyes upon this sheep that was lost. O glance of wonderful power: silent, but oh, how full of meaning. Well did Peter understand that language and the message of that look. Vain was Jesus's prophecy of the cock crow to arouse Peter, but not the clamor of those eyes. They do not merely speak, these eyes of Christ, they work; the tears of Peter prove it, tears which flow not so much from the eyes of Peter as from the eyes of Christ.

And now, after these injuries, consider the blows our Savior received at the pillar. The judge, seeing that he could not appease the fury of that hellish crowd, decided to inflict on him so terrible a flagellation that it might suffice to satisfy the rage of those cruel hearts, and that, contented with this, they might no longer press for his death. Enter now in spirit, O my soul, into the praetorium of Pilate. Hold yourself ready to weep, for you will indeed have need of tears at what you are about to see and hear. See how inhumanly these vile and cruel executioners

14. Lk 22:61.

strip our Savior of his garments, and how, with great humility, he allows himself to be thus despoiled without opening his mouth or answering a single word to all the insults they shower upon him. See how they fasten his holy body to a pillar, that thus they may be free to wound it just as they please, no matter where or how. See the Lord of angels quite alone there, in the midst of these cruel executioners, without friends of any kind, or protectors to take his part, not even encountering from any eyes a glance of compassion. Watch how they begin, at once, with unmeasured cruelty, to lay their rods and cords upon that most sensitive body. Blow succeeds blow, bruise is added to bruise, gash to gash. Soon you will see this most holy body become a livid mass of wounds, the skin torn away, the blood gushing forth and streaming down on all sides. But what must it be, above all, to see that great open wound between the shoulders where the blows fall thickest?

The scourging over, watch our Lord clothing himself again: from one corner of the hall to another he goes, picking up his garments in the presence of those cruel executioners, for none will serve or help him, none will offer anything to soothe or refresh him, as was usually done for those thus covered with wounds.

All these mysteries are well worthy of deep devotion, gratitude and thought.

Thursday: The Crowning with Thorns, the *Ecce Homo*, and the Carrying of the Cross

Today we must think of the crowning with thorns, the *Ecce Homo,* and how the Savior, pleading, carries the Cross. In the

Song of Solomon the Spouse thus invites us to the consideration of these sad mysteries: *Go forth, O daughters of Zion and behold King Solomon, with the crown with which his mother crowned him on the day of his wedding, on the day of the gladness of his heart.*[15]

O my soul, what are you doing? My heart, what do you think? My tongue, why are you silent? O my most sweet Saviour, when I open my eyes and gaze upon this sorrowful scene as it unfolds before me, my heart is broken with grief. Are they not then sufficient, Lord, those blows that are past, the death which is to come, and so much blood poured out already, that these thorns need to be driven in by force, and draw from the head the blood the scourging has spared? To appreciate something of this so sorrowful a mystery, place first before your eyes, O my soul, the image of this Lord as he was before, and the grandeur of his virtues, and then contrast his present state. See the splendor of his beauty, the gentleness of his eyes, the sweetness of his words, his air of authority, and with it all, his meekness, his calmness, and that peculiar aspect of his which commanded so much veneration.

After having studied and appreciated so wasted a figure, turn your eyes upon what is now before you, a figure derisively clad in purple, the reed as a royal scepter in his hand, and upon his head this diadem of terror. His eyes are closed, his face as of one dead, and all his person covered with blood and fouled with spittle. View him within and without, the heart seared with sorrow, the body torn with wounds, abandoned by his disciples, pursued by the Jews, mocked by the

15. Song 3:11.

soldiers, scorned by the high priests, turned back by a wicked king, accused unjustly and deprived of all good will. Do not think of all this as over and done, but as something present; no sorrow, this, of another's, but your very own. Put yourself in the place of him who suffers: think what you would suffer yourself if, in so sensitive a part as the head, many and sharp-pointed thorns were pressed in so deeply as to penetrate to the bone. Thorns indeed! Why, the simple prick of a pin is scarcely endurable! What then must this head have suffered, itself so sensitive, and yet subjected to such a string of torments?

The crowning with thorns over, and the mocking of the Savior finished, the judge takes him by the hand, and, all battered as he is, brings him face to face with the furious crowd, saying, *Ecce Homo: Behold the Man.* It was as much as to say: If it was through envy you sought his death, see him now, an object of envy no longer, but of pity. You feared he might make himself king: see him now so disfigured he hardly carries the semblance of a man. From these torn hands what do you dread? From this racked frame what more do you demand?

From this you may form an idea, O my soul, of what the Savior looked like, since the judge thought it enough to expose that figure to soften even such as his enemies. You may well understand how evil a thing it is to have no Christian compassion for the sufferings of Christ, since they were such as might—so the judge thought—have induced tenderness even into those proud hearts.

Pilate, seeing how all that had been already inflicted on that most holy Lamb had not yet sufficed to calm the fury of his enemies, entered into the praetorium and seated himself on his throne to pronounce the final sentence. Even now the cross was ready at the gates, and this terrible banner appeared aloft, menacing the Savior's head. The cruel sentence is pronounced and promulgated. His enemies add cruelty to cruelty, for they lay upon these shoulders, bruised and torn by blows, the plank of the cross. The gentle Savior accepts this burden, laden with all our sins. Even more, with unbounded charity and obedience, he embraces it for love of us.

The innocent Isaac advances towards the place of sacrifice bearing this heavy burden upon his failing shoulders. A large crowd follows him, and many holy women accompany him weeping. Who, indeed, would not shed tears at seeing the King of angels moving forward step by step, with this weighty load upon him, his knees trembling, his body bent, the eyes almost closed, the face all smeared with blood, and this garland about his head, in the midst of a shameless clamor and of outcries against him.

And now, my soul, turn your eyes away for a little while from this cruel spectacle. Hasten, with all speed and sobbing breath and weeping eyes, and seek the Virgin's house. When found, cast yourself at her feet, and begin to say to her in accents of grief: "Our Lady of the angels, queen of heaven, gate of paradise, advocate of the world, refuge of sinners, salvation of the just, joy of the saints, mistress of all virtues, mirror of purity, ensign of chastity, model of patience and sum of all perfections: Woe is me, my Lady, that my sight should have been preserved to see this hour. How shall I live longer now that my eyes have witnessed what has just passed before them? What further need of words: I come from your only

Son, and my Lord; and he was in the midst of friends of mine, carrying the cross on which he is to be crucified."

Who can fathom now the Virgin's grief? Her soul faints away; her face and all her virginal body is bathed in a deadly sweat, which would indeed have borne her life away had not the will of God preserved her for a yet greater martyrdom and a more glorious crown. She goes forth, this Virgin, in search of her Son. The longing to see him gives back to her the strength of which grief had deprived her. She hears from afar the clash of arms, the tramp of many feet and the voices of the city criers making proclamation. Soon she catches sight on high of the lanceheads and halberds, and perceives on the ground drops and traces of blood, which suffice, without other guide, to show where her Son has passed. Nearer and nearer does she draw to this loved Son of hers; she lifts up her eyes, darkened with sorrow and the shadow of death, to catch a glimpse, if she can, of one who so loved her soul. Oh, what dread and longing are mingled in Mary's heart: at one moment longing to see him, at the next shrinking back with dread lest she might see a sight so lamentable.

At length she arrives at a spot where she can see him: one upon the other they gaze, these two lights of heaven: to the inmost heart do their looks penetrate, revealing what stirs to the depths their compassionate souls. Silent are their lips, but the Mother's heart spoke, and her very gentle Son made answer: "Why have you come here, my beloved, my very dearest and my Mother? Your sorrow increases mine, your torments torture me. Return, my Mother, return to your house. Your modesty and virginal purity are ill suited to the company of murderers and thieves." Such, and others more touching still, were the words which these hearts, so full of compassion, addressed one to the other: and thus was the toilsome journey completed to the place of crucifixion.

Friday: The Crucifixion and the Seven Words

Today we must contemplate the mystery of the Cross, and our Lord's seven words. Arouse yourself now, O my soul, and set yourself to consider the mystery of the holy cross. Its fruit has made good the evil caused by the poisoned fruit of Eden's forbidden tree.

Firstly see our Savior, arrived now at the place of execution. His depraved enemies, desirous of making his death more shameful still, strip him of all his garments, including the inner tunic which was all woven in one piece, without seam. Mark with what meekness this most innocent Lamb allows himself to be despoiled, without opening his mouth, or breathing one single word against those who were thus maltreating him. Rather is it with good will that he consents to be stripped of his garments, to bear the shame of nakedness, for it is thus that he may reclothe, far better than with the leaves of a fig tree, the nakedness into which we fell by sin.

Certain learned writers tell us that, to remove our Lord's tunic, they took off, with great cruelty, the crown of thorns upon his head; and, once he was stripped, replaced it again, driving in the thorns deeply for the second time, and thus causing him the greatest suffering. It is quite conceivable that this cruelty was practiced upon Christ together with all those other ones, and some so unusual which they made him undergo during the course of his Passion. Then the tunic was already clinging close to the wounds caused by the scourging, and the blood had congealed and become attached to the garment, so that, when they stripped him—so completely were these evil men devoid of pity—they tore it off with one wrench and with such force that they opened again and renewed all these wounds of the scourging. This way his holy body lay open and, as it were, flayed on all sides, leaving nothing but one vast wound, pouring out blood from every part.

Consider here, O my soul, the grandeur of the divine bounty and mercy which both shine forth in this mystery with such resplendence. He who spreads the sky with clouds and the fields with flowers and beauty, is himself despoiled of his garments. Think of the cold this holy body must have suffered; all shattered as it was, and stripped, not merely of clothes, but of skin, and open on every side with gaping wounds. St. Peter, the previous night, clad, as he was, and standing by a fire, yet felt the cold. How much more must this most sensitive body have suffered, all nakedness and wounds?

Consider how our Savior was nailed to the Cross. Think of the anguish he must have endured as these thick, bent nails pass through the most sensitive and delicate parts of his frame. Think of the Virgin Mary who sees with her eyes, and hears with her ears the blows, hard and cruel, as they fall one by one upon these divine limbs. Truly these hammer blows and these nails that pierce her son's hands, wound yet more the mother's heart.

Now how they raise the Cross on high and make ready to drop it into the hole which has been prepared for it, and how these cruel executioners, at the given moment, let it fall with a jerk, causing the whole sacred body to shake violently in the air, and thus enlarging the wounds of the nails with intolerable pain.

O my Savior and Redeemer, what heart, though it be of stone, will not share this torment? For indeed, on that day, the very rocks were rent asunder on beholding your sufferings on the cross. *The cords of death encompassed me, the torrents of perdition assailed me.*[16] Further: *I sink in deep mire, where there is no foothold.*[17] And Matthew: *My God, my God, why hast thou forsaken me?*[18]

What do you look for from men, O Lord? Your enemies cry out against you, your friends break your heart, your soul is troubled, and, for love of me, you admit no consolation. Stubborn indeed were my sins; the evidence for your expiation. I behold you, O my King, fastened to this beam, with nought to sustain you but these three nails of iron; they alone support your sacred body; there is no rest for you but on them. When you allow the body's weight to rest upon the feet, you only widen more the wounds of the feet with the nails that pierce them. Would you use the hands as a support? Then the whole weight of the body serves but to enlarge also these wounds in the hands. What cushion supports your sacred head, tormented and weakened by the crown of thorns, what cushion is there to support it! O how willingly, Virgin most serene, would your arms have given this support, but no arms of yours can serve here, only those of the cross. Upon them will this sacred head recline, when it would be at rest; and the only solace it will have will be to dig in deeper yet the thorns into the skull.

The presence of the Mother increased still more the sorrows of the Son. His heart rent within, no less was his sacred

16. Ps 18 (17):5.

17. Ps 69 (68): 2.

18. Mt 27:46.

body rent without. O good Jesus, there are, indeed, two crosses for you this day, one for the body, and one for the soul; one, the outward passion; the other, compassion. The one pierces the body with iron nails; the other, your most holy soul with nails of sorrow. Who can declare, O good Jesus, what you felt as you recognized the anguish of that most holy soul which clung so closely with you to the cross, when you saw this devoted soul pierced through and through with a sword of sorrow, when you turned towards her those bleeding eyes and gazed on that sacred face enveloped in the bitterness of death, and watched the anguish of that soul so near to death, to worse than death, and the streaming tears that flowed from those eyes most pure, and when you heard the groans drawn from that sacred heart under so desperate a weight of grief.

Now you may consider the seven words, or expressions, pronounced by our Lord from the cross. Of these, the first was: *Father, forgive them; for they know not what they do.*[19] The second was addressed to the thief: *Today you will be with me in paradise,*[20] and the third to his most holy Mother: *Woman, behold your Son.*[21] The fourth: *I thirst.*[22] The fifth: *My God, My God, why has thou forsaken me?*[23] The sixth: *It is finished.*[24] The seventh: *Father, into thy hands I commit my spirit.*[25]

---

19. Lk 23:34.
20. Lk 23:43.
21. Jn 19:26.
22. Jn 19:28.
23. Mt 27:46.
24. Jn 19:30.
25. Lk 23:46.

Consider, O my soul, with what charitable words he commends his enemies to the Father, with what mercy he welcomes the thief who recognized him, with what immense love he recommends his pious Mother to the beloved disciple, with what thirsting zeal he witnesses to his longing for the salvation of men, in what sorrowful tones he pronounces his prayer and lays his griefs before the divine Majesty, how to the end he remains in the most perfect submission to the Father, and how finally he recommends his soul to him, and resigns himself completely into his most holy keeping.

Each one of these words teaches a lesson of virtue. The first recommends to us charity towards our enemies. The second, mercy towards sinners. The third, duty towards our parents. The fourth, the desire of our neighbor's salvation. The fifth, prayer in the midst of tribulations and abandonment by God. The sixth, the virtue of obedience and perseverance. The seventh, perfect resignation into the hands of God, in whom lies our whole perfection.

Saturday: The Piercing with the Lance, the Taking Down from the Cross, the Sorrows of Mary and the Burial

Today, think of the Savior pierced with a lance, of the taking down from the cross, of the tears of our Lady, and of the laying in the tomb.

Consider how our Savior has now expired upon the cross, and accomplished the desires of his cruel enemies who wished to see him die. But, for all that, the flame of their wrath is not extinguished. They still seek to wreak vengeance upon him. They set furiously upon these holy relics, dividing among themselves and casting lots for his garments, and piercing his sacred side with the cruel blow of a lance. O savage servants! O hearts of iron! Did the sufferings of the living body seem so slight to you, that you would not even let him be in death? What rage or enmity so great that it is not sated at sight of the enemy dead before its face? Lift up for a moment your cruel eyes, and see this lifeless figure, these sightless eyes, this pallid countenance, this shadowed bitterness of death. Are you then harder than iron or the diamond, that this sight does not soften you?

And now the soldier advances, lance in hand, and, with all his strength, plunges it into the bare breast of the Saviour. The cross shakes in the air with the force of the blow, and there gush forth water and blood for the healing of the world's sin. O river flowing out from Paradise, and inundating all the earth with your streams! O wound in the sacred side, caused by love for men rather than by the iron of the lance! O gateway of heaven, and avenue of paradise, refuge and fortified tower, sanctuary of the just, last resting place of the pilgrim, nest for the spotless doves and flowered bed of the Spouse of Solomon! Hail, O wound in that precious side, which rends devout hearts; wound, which pierces the souls of the just; rose of beauty unspeakable; ruby of priceless worth; door into the heart of Christ; witness of his love and pledge of eternal life!

Consider, now, how at the close of this same day, those two holy persons arrived, Joseph and Nicodemus. They set their ladders to the cross, and lifted down in their arms the body of the Savior. When the Virgin saw that an end had come to the torments, and that this sacred body was being lowered to the ground, she prepared herself to assure it a safe refuge in her arms, and from the arms of the cross to her own.

So with great humility she asked these noble personages that, as she had not been able to bid her Son adieu, nor to receive his last embrace, as he died upon the cross, that she might now be allowed to approach. She begged them not to add to her desolation, and, though his enemies would not leave him to her living, that his friends would not deny him to her in death. The Virgin then takes him in her arms, and what words can voice all she felt?

O angels of peace, weep with this holy Virgin: weep, ye skies; ye stars of heaven, weep; and all you creatures of earth join with Mary in her lamentations. The Mother embraces that shattered body, gathers it closely to her breast—she has no strength but for that—and lays her head amid the thorns of that sacred brow. Body to body, the figure of this most holy Mother is stained with the Son's blood, and that of the Son steeped in the Mother's tears. O gentle Mother, is this then, truly, your most sweet child? Is this he whom you conceived in such glory and bore with such joy? Where are the joys of the past? Your delights of bygone days, where are they? Is this that mirror of beauty on which you gazed?

All around were weeping; the holy women were in tears, and those noble men, heaven and earth were weeping, and all creatures shared the Virgin's tears. The holy evangelist wept too, and embraced the body of his Master, saying: "O good Master, O my Lord: who now will guide me? Before whom shall I lay my doubts? On whose breast shall I recline? Who will share with me the secrets of heaven? What staggering change is this? Last night you pressed me to your Sacred

Heart, and gave the joy of life to me; and now I repay so great a gift by holding you lifeless in my arms. Is that the face I gazed on, transfigured on Mount Tabor? Is this the figure which then was brighter than the sun at noon?"

That holy woman, a sinner once, wept also, and embracing the Savior's feet exclaimed: "O light of my eyes and healing of my soul, wearied with sin, as you see me, who will now receive me, who will heal my wounds, who will answer for me, who will defend me from the Pharisees? O how different were these feet when I washed them, and you welcomed me as I knelt! O beloved of my heart, who will tell me that I may die with you? O life of my soul, how can I say I love you, since, though holding you dead before my eyes, I yet live?"

Thus all that holy company wept and lamented, bathing and cleansing with their tears this sacred body. As the moment of burial approached, they enveloped the holy body in a white windingsheet, covered the head with a linen cloth, and then, placing it on a stretcher, made their way towards the tomb. There they laid this precious treasure; the sepulchre was closed with a stone, and the Mother's heart with a dark cloud of sorrow. There, for the second time, she separates herself from her Son and, once again, feels her loneliness; there she sees herself despoiled of all her good; there, where her treasure is, her heart lies buried.

Sunday: The Descent into Limbo, the Appearances of our Lord and the Ascension

Today you may think of the descent of our Lord into Limbo, of the appearance to our Lady, to Mary Magdalen, and to the disciples; and finally of the mystery of the glorious Ascension.

As for the first point, consider how great, on this day, is the joy of the holy patriarchs in Limbo, at the coming and presence among them of their liberator, and what thanks and praise they offer him for a salvation so long hoped and desired. Those who come back to Spain from the East Indies tell us that they look on the time spent on the voyage as well employed on account of the delight they feel when they reach land. If this is true of such a journey as that, and after an exile of one or two years, what must it be, after an exile of three or four thousand years, when the day comes on which so great a salvation is secured, and on which they reach a safe harbor?

Consider, also, the joy which the most holy Virgin experienced when, on this day, she received the visit of her risen Son. Certainly, as it was she who felt most deeply the sorrows of his Passion, so it is she who will taste most fully the joy of his Resurrection. What must her feelings have been as, before her, she beheld her Son, living and glorious, attended by all those holy patriarchs risen with him? What does she do? What does she say? How she embraces him and kisses him, tears falling all the while from those devoted eyes. Oh, the longing to go with him, if this grace might be granted her!

Think of the joy of the holy Marys, and especially of her who lingered weeping at the tomb, waiting for the Beloved of her soul, that she might cast herself at his feet and speak with him living and risen whom in death she had longed for and sought. Note well that, after his Mother, it is to her he first appears, for she loved him more than the rest, and sought him with more persevering care and more abundant tears. So you may hold it as certain that you too will speak with God if you seek him with tears and care like hers.

Consider how he appeared, in the guise of a pilgrim, to the disciples who were going to Emmaus; with what affability he joins them, with what familiarity he accompanies them, how gently he conceals his identity from them, and, then, with what love he reveals himself to them and leaves them with a sweetness as of honey upon their lips. Let your conversation resemble theirs; speak with compassionate sorrow, as did they, of the anguish and pain of Christ, and you may be sure his accompanying presence will never fail you, if you bear within you always the memory of him.

Consider how our Lord delayed his ascension into heaven for forty days, during which time he frequently appeared to his disciples, and taught them, and spoke with them of the kingdom of God. He did not then ascend to heaven and separate himself from them, before they were ready themselves to ascend in spirit with him. This shows us that often the actual presence of Christ i.e., the consoling *feeling* of devotion—is withdrawn from those who, rising high in spiritual flight, are thereby secured the more against danger. The providence of God is wonderfully evident here, and his manner of dealing with his own at various times. He coaxes the weak with favors, the strong he puts to the test. For the tiny ones there is milk; the bigger ones are weaned. Some he consoles, others he reproves, treating each one according to the measure of his progress. Consequently he who is regaled with devotion should not presume, for favor is a sign of his weakness, and one in desolation should not lose courage, since it is often a sign of strength.

In the presence of his disciples, and while they were *looking on,* he ascends to heaven, that they may be witnesses of these mysteries; and no better witness to God's works is he who knows of them by experience. If you would truly know how good God is, how gracious and gentle with his own, and of what kind is the virtue and efficacy of his grace, of his love, of his providence and of his consolations, ask it of those who have experienced it, and they will give you a very convincing testimony.[26]

The Savior also wished his disciples to see him mounting to heaven that they might follow him with their eyes and in spirit, that they might realize the parting, and experience some loneliness from his absence, such being the best preparation for the reception of his grace. Elisha demanded of Elijah his spirit, and this good master replied: *If you see me when I am taken from you, you shall have what you have asked.*[27] The heirs of the spirit of Christ will be those whose love will make them feel the departure of Christ, who will suffer from his absence, and who, throughout this exile, will be forever sighing after his presence. *If you see me as I am being taken from you; it shall be so (inheriting a double share of the spirit) for you; but if you do not see me, it shall not be so.*[28]

What was the loneliness, the grief, the lamentations and tears of the most holy Virgin, of the beloved disciple, of St. Mary Magdalen and of all the apostles as they watched fade away from their sight the One who had stolen their hearts?

---

26. As was precisely the case with St. Teresa of Avila when she sought St. Peter's counsel and advice. St. Teresa, *Autobiography,* chapter 30.

27. 2 Kings 2:10.

28. St. Ignatius, *The Spiritual Exercises: Fourth Week, First Contemplation.*

Yet we are told that they went back to Jerusalem with great joy, for they loved him much; and indeed, it was this same love which, though it made them feel the parting, led them, on the other hand, to rejoice in his glory; for true love seeks not itself, but rather the object of its love.

It remains to consider with what glory and joy and hymns of praise this noble victor was received into his heavenly city, and how festive was his reception. Men and angels unite together and move forward towards this noble city, once again to inhabit a long-deserted spot. Christ, in his most sacred humanity, advances above them all, and goes to seat himself at the Father's right hand. How much can we ponder here. We see how well employed are those who labour for the love of God, and how he who humbles himself and suffers more than any other is glorified and raised higher than all. Thus those enamored of true glory know well the road they must take to arrive there, which is to go down that they may ascend, and to submit themselves to all, that they may be elevated above all.

5

Six Parts which May Enter into the Exercise of Prayer

SUCH, THEN, CHRISTIAN READER, are the meditations which you may consider during each day of the week, and thus there should be no lack of matter for reflection. It should be borne in mind, however, that the meditation may be preceded and followed by certain other related and appropriate exercises.

In the first place, before beginning the meditation, it is necessary to prepare the heart for this holy exercise, as one might tune up a guitar before playing on it.

Then comes the reading of the meditation for that day, according to the order for the days of the week. This is certainly necessary for beginners, and until one is familiar with subjects of meditation.

The meditation may be followed by a devout act of thanksgiving for benefits received, and by an offering of our whole life and of that of Christ our Savior.

Finally comes the petition—prayer, strictly so called—in which we ask for what we need, and for our salvation, together with that of our neighbor and of the whole Church.

These six acts[1] may well find a place in prayer. Among other advantages they serve to furnish abundant matter for carrying the exercise forward, and to offer various kinds of nourishment, so that one has a choice, and if he lose the thread of the meditation at any point, another is at hand on which to continue.

All these steps, and in the given order, are not always necessary, but still they serve to guide beginners, by giving them a definite order to follow and a scheme by which they may direct themselves. Again, in all I have said so far, I would not be considered as laying down a permanent rule or general law, for my intention is not to lay down rules, but to introduce newcomers into this path. Once they have entered upon it, the rest will come from use and experience and, most of all, from the Holy Spirit.

---

1. The six are: preparation, reading, meditation, thanksgiving, offering and petition. Clearly we have here the familiar and simplest of all *schemes* of mental prayer, which groups the exercise into three sections (1) the preparation, (2) the *discursive* part, *i.e.*, reading or thinking about the subject-matter, (3) the *affections*, of which St. Peter enumerates three.

6

The Preparation Required before Prayer

NOW IT WILL BE USEFUL to describe each one of the above-mentioned steps, the first being, the preparation.

At the place of prayer, kneel or stand, or with arms extended in the form of a cross, or prostrate on the ground, or seated, should you be unable to manage otherwise. (These postures were not unusual in a monastery, but would be inappropriate in a public church or chapel, especially when others are present).

Then begin with the sign of the Cross, and get your imagination under control, withdrawing it from the affairs of daily life, raising up your soul and considering how our Lord is watching you. Maintain in yourself the same attention and respect as if you saw him actually present. Make a general act of contrition, if it is the morning meditation, and say the *Confiteor*, the *I confess*. If it is in the evening, examine your conscience on all your thoughts, words, actions and omissions, and on your forgetfulness of our Lord, grieving over the defects of that day and of all your life, humbling yourself before the majesty of God in whose presence you stand. Say these words of Abraham: *I have taken upon myself to speak to the Lord, I who am but dust and ashes.*[1] Then you will say these verses of the Psalm:

> To thee I lift up my eyes, O thou who art enthroned
> in the heavens.
> Behold as the eyes of servants look to the hands of
> their master,
> As the eyes of a maid to the hands of her mistress,
> So our eyes look to the Lord our God,
> Until he have mercy on us.
> Have mercy upon us, O Lord, have mercy upon us.[2]

> Glory be to the Father . . .

Moreover, as we are not able, of ourselves, to frame one single good thought, but *our sufficiency is from God,*[3] and as no one can invoke worthily the name of Jesus without the help of the Holy Spirit, let us say:

> Come, most sweet Spirit, and send forth from heaven a ray of your light. Come, father of the poor: come, giver of gifts: come, illuminator of hearts. Come, best of consolers, gentle guest of the soul, and rest thereof. You are our repose in toil, our refreshment in the heat of the day, our consolation in the midst of tears. O most blessed light, fill the hearts of the faithful.

1. Gen 18:27.
2. Ps 123 (122): 1–3.
3. 2 Cor 3:5.

V. Send forth your Spirit and they shall be created.

R. And you shall renew the face of the earth.

O God, who has taught the hearts of the faithful by the light of the Holy Spirit, grant us in the same Spirit to be always truly wise, and ever to rejoice in his consolation, through Christ our Lord. Amen.

These prayers said, beg our Lord to give you the grace to remain there with that attention and devotion, with that interior recollection, with that fear and reverence which befit this sovereign majesty. May you spend this time of prayer in such manner as to come forth with renewed strength and ready for everything in his service. Prayer which does not at once produce this fruit is very imperfect and almost valueless.[4]

---

4. See *The Spiritual Exercises of St. Ignatius: Additions,* First Week, iii and iv, www.catholicspiritualdirection.org/spiritualexercises.pdf.

7

The Reading

THE PREPARATION FINISHED, now comes the reading of the meditation which is to form the prayer's subject matter. This must not be done hurriedly nor in cursory fashion, but with attention and calm, applying not merely one's intelligence, so as to understand what is read, but, above all, that the will delight in it. And when one discovers some moving passage, one should pause so as to appreciate it better. The reading should not be very long. Thus a longer time will be available for the meditation, which is all the more profitable in proportion as one ponders more leisurely on what is read and enters more devoutly into its spirit.

However, should the heart be too distracted for prayer, one may delay a little longer over the reading, or combine reading with meditation, by reading a passage and then meditating on it, reading another and meditating on that, and so on. The mind, fixed on the words, does not so easily wander away on all sides, as when free and unrestricted: but it is better still to resist and scorn these distracting thoughts, and to go on struggling in the work of prayer (like Jacob of old, who strove throughout the night).[1]

1. Gen 32:24.

The contest will cease in the end, and victory will be won, and our Lord will give us devotion, or some even greater grace, for he never refuses himself to such as combat faithfully.

8

The Meditation

AFTER THE READING COMES the meditation on what we have just read. Some subjects of this meditation may be visualized by the imagination, such as all the scenes in the Life and Passion of Christ, the Last Judgement, Hell and Heaven. Others pertain to the understanding rather than to the imagination. For example, the benefits of God, his goodness and mercy, or any other of his perfections which we may choose to consider. This kind of meditation is called *intellectual,* and the other *imaginative.* We are likely, in these exercises, to use one or other, as the subject matter demands.

When the meditation is *imaginative* we must figure each detail as it actually exists, or actually happens, and must consider it as taking place in the very spot where we are, and in our presence. Such a representation will make our consideration and appreciation of the mystery more vivid. It will be even better to imagine all as taking place within our own hearts. If cities and kingdoms can find a place there, how much more a representation of these mysteries. This will help a great deal in keeping the soul recollected, by occupying it within itself (like the bee in the hive, busy over its honey); for to go in thought to Jerusalem, and to meditate upon these mysteries where they took place, is something which usually causes headache and weariness. No one, consequently, should fix the imagination too intently on what he is considering, lest so forceful an application should strain his natural powers.

9

The Thanksgiving

After the meditation comes the act of thanksgiving. The soul should take occasion of the meditation just concluded to thank our Lord for the benefit conferred in the considered mystery. Thus if the meditation has been on the Passion we ought to thank our Lord for having, with so much toil, redeemed us; if it has been on sin, for having waited so long for our repentance; if on the miseries of this life, for having spared us so many; if on the moment of death, for delivering us from the dangers, and for having waited for us to repent; if on the glory of heaven, for having made it so perfect; and so on.

To these benefits should be joined all those others of which we have spoken already: creation, preservation, redemption, vocation, etc. Thus each one should thank our Lord, for having made him in his image and likeness; for giving him memory with which he may call God to mind, and the understanding with which to know him, and the will with which to love him; for giving him an angel to guard him from so many pains and perils, from many mortal sins and from dying in sin—which is nothing less than a delivery from eternal death; for having deigned himself to assume our nature and to die for us; for having caused him to be born of

Christian parents, for the gift of holy baptism, for the gift of grace here and the promise of glory, and for having received him as his adopted son; for having fitted him out with arms, in the sacrament of Confirmation, with which to combat the devil, the world and the flesh; for having given us himself in the sacrament of the Altar, and for having placed within reach the sacrament of Penance where grace, lost through mortal sin, may be recovered; and, finally, for the many good inspirations he has given in the past, and still gives, and for the assistance accorded us to pray and work well and to persevere in the good. To these benefits join those others, general and particular, which you recognize as having been received from our Lord. For these and all others, as well open as hidden, render as much thanks as possible, and summon all created things in heaven and on earth to help you in this work. To this end you may recite this canticle:

> Bless the Lord, all ye works of the Lord,
> Sing praise to him and highly exalt him forever.[1]

Or this Psalm

> Bless the Lord, O my soul, and all that is within me,
> bless his holy name!
> Bless the Lord, O my soul, and forget not all his benefits.
> Who forgives all your iniquity, who heals all your diseases,
> Who redeems your life from the Pit, who crowns you
> with steadfast love and mercy.[2]

---

1. Dan 3:35.
2. Ps 103 (102):1–4.

10

The Offering

WHEN WE HAVE GIVEN HEARTFELT thanks to our Lord for all these benefits, there naturally rises within us that feeling which the prophet David expressed in the words, *What shall I render to the Lord for all his bounty to me?*[1] A man may, in some measure, satisfy this desire by giving, on his part, and offering to God everything that he has and is able to offer.

To this end he should first offer himself as his servant forever, resigning and placing himself in his hands so that he may do with him whatever he would, in time and in eternity. Let him offer, at the same time, all his words, actions, thoughts and toils, all he may have to bear and suffer, that all may be to the honor and glory of God's holy name.

Second, offer to the Father all the merits and good works of his Son, all the toils that he obediently underwent from the crib to the cross, for it is all our treasure and heritage which he has bequeathed us in the New Testament by which he has made us heirs to all this great wealth.

For just as what is given me by grace is no less mine than what I win by my own efforts, so the merits and rights which

1. Ps 115:12.

he has given me belong to me as much as if I had myself sweated and labored to secure them. Thus may a man make this second offering no less than the former, counting up as his own all the services, work, and virtues of that most holy life: his obedience, his patience, his humility, his loyalty, his love, his mercy and all the rest. This is the richest and most precious offering we can possibly make to God.[2]

2. *The Spiritual Exercises of St. Ignatius*, the well-known prayer *Sume et suscipe, in the Contemplation to Gain Love: Fourth Week*. See www.sacred-texts.com/chr/seil/seil35.htm.

11

The Petition

Special Prayer for the Love of God

AFTER MAKING SO RICH an offering we may confidently anticipate a prompt recompense. First, with a deep sentiment of charity and with zeal for the honor of our Lord, let us beg that all peoples and nations of the world may know, praise and adore him as their own true God and Lord, saying, with all our hearts, these words of the prophet: *Let the peoples praise thee, O God; let all the peoples praise thee!*[1]

Pray also for the heads of the Church—the Pope, cardinals and bishops—and for all the other ministers and lower prelates, that our Lord may direct and enlighten them in such a way that they may lead all men to know and obey their Creator. Also, as St. Paul counsels us, we should pray for our leaders, and all holding similar positions of dignity, that through their foresight we may pass quiet and tranquil lives. This is well pleasing to God, our Lord, *who desires all men to be saved and to come to the knowledge of the truth.*[2]

1. Ps 67 (66):5.

2. 1 Tim 2:2.

Let us pray also for all the members of his Mystical Body; for the good, that our Lord may preserve them; for sinners, that he may convert them; for the dead, that he may mercifully free them from all toil, and lead them to the repose of eternal life. Let us ask also for all poor people, and infirm, for those in prison and captives, that, through the merits of his Son, God may help them and deliver them from evil.

Having prayed for our neighbor, let us also pray for ourselves. Each one's individual needs will make clear his requests, if one knows oneself well. However, that there may be no uncertainty in this matter, the following are the graces for which we may beg.

First, through the merits and sufferings of our Lord, let us beg pardon and contrition for all our sins, and especially let us ask for help against all those passions and vices towards which we incline the most and are most tempted, revealing all our wounds to the heavenly Physician that he may heal and cure them with the unction of his grace.

Then, second, let us ask for those very lofty and noble virtues in which is contained the sum of all Christian perfection—faith, hope, love, fear, humility, patience, obedience, courage to face every toil, poverty of spirit, contempt of the world, discretion, purity of intention, and other similar virtues—which lie at the summit of this spiritual edifice. Faith is the primary root of all Christian life; hope is the prop and remedy in all the temptations of life; love is the culminating point of all Christian perfection; the fear of God is the beginning of true wisdom; humility is the foundation of all virtues; patience is a shield against the blows and assaults of the enemy; obedience is a most agreeable offering, by which a man offers himself in sacrifice to God; discretion is the eye of the soul to enlighten and direct her in every path, and courage is her arm for the accomplishment of every labor, and purity of intention refers and directs all our actions towards God.

Third, let us also pray for those other virtues, though which, less important, help, nevertheless, to preserve the latter—temperance in eating and drinking, restraint of the tongue, custody of the senses, a modest and composed deportment, charming in manner, good example towards one's neighbor, rigor and austerity towards oneself, and other such good qualities.

After this conclude with the prayer for the love of God; dwell upon this, occupy with this the greater part of your time, demand of our Lord this virtue ardent longing, for herein lies all our good. Thus may you pray:

Special prayer for the love of God

Above all these virtues, give me, O Lord, your grace, that I may love you with my whole heart, with my whole soul, with all my strength and with my whole being, for thus you bid me do. Oh, you are all my hope and all my glory, my one refuge, my whole joy! O best beloved of all: spouse emblossomed, honeyed and sweet: O sweetness of my heart, life of my soul, joyous resting place of my spirit! O day of eternity, beautiful and bright, my innermost light serene; flowering paradise of my heart; my Creator, most lovable and all-sufficient for me!

Make ready, O my God and Lord, a pleasing dwelling place within me for yourself, that according to the promise of your holy word, you may come to me and rest with me. Mortify in me all that is displeasing to your sight, and renew me according to your own heart. Wound, Lord, my inmost soul with the arrows of your love, and inebriate it with the wine of your perfect charity. Ah! when will that be? When shall I please you in all things? When shall I be dead to all in me that displeases you? When shall I be wholly yours? When shall I cease to be my own? When shall no one but yourself live in me? When shall I love you most ardently? When will your love's flame wholly enkindle me? When shall I be wholly softened and carried away by your most potent sweetness? When will you open yourself to this poor mendicant, and reveal to him your most lovely kingdom, which is within me, which is yourself, with all your treasures? When will you ravish me and sweep me off, transport me and hide me in yourself, so that nothing of myself appears anymore? When, quit of these impeding chains, will you make me a spirit with you that nothing may any more separate me from you?

O beloved, beloved, beloved of my soul! O sweetness, sweetness of my heart! Hearken to me, Lord, not for any merits of mine, but because of your infinite bounty. Teach me, enlighten me, guide and help me in all things so that nothing may be done or said but what is pleasing in your sight. O my God, my loved one, and the innermost good of my soul! O love, so sweet to me! O delight, so great for me! O my strength, help me; my light, guide me!

O God of my heart! Why do you not bestow yourself on one so poor? You fill earth and sky, and yet my heart is empty. You clothe the lilies of the field, you feed the little birds, you support the worms; why do you forget me, I who have forgotten all things for you? Late have I known you, infinite goodness! Late have I loved you, beauty, so ancient and so new! How sad the time when I loved you not! How sad, myself, when I knew you not, how blind when I did not see you! You are within me and I sought you without! But since at long last I have found you, suffer me not, Lord, in your clemency divine, ever again to leave you.

Since it pleases you most, and most deeply touches your heart, to have eyes that know how to gaze upon you, give me, Lord, such eyes as these that I may contemplate you: eyes of the dove, simple; eyes chaste and modest; eyes humble and loving; eyes filled with devotion and with tears; eyes attentive and discerning, to know your will and do it. May I, gazing upon you with such eyes as these, be myself regarded with your eyes which looked upon Peter when you led him to weep for his sin; with those eyes with which you looked upon the prodigal son when you went forward to welcome him and give him the kiss of peace; with those eyes which you turned towards the Publican, when he dared not raise his own towards heaven; with those eyes with which you gazed upon the Magdalen, when she washed your feet with her tears; those eyes with which you gazed upon the Spouse, in the Canticles, saying to her: *Behold, you are beautiful, my love; behold, you are beautiful; your eyes are doves.*[3] Thus, well pleased with the eyes and with the beauty of my soul, adorn me with those virtues and graces with which I shall always appear beautiful in your sight.

O most high, most clement and most benign Trinity, Father, Son and Holy Spirit, one only true God, teach me, direct me, help me, Lord, in all things. O Father, all-powerful, with the greatness of your infinite power center and fix my memory in yourself, and fill it with holy and devout thoughts. O Son, most holy, with your eternal wisdom enlighten my understanding, and adorn it with the knowledge of sovereign truth and of my own extreme baseness. O Holy Spirit, Love of the Father and of the Son; pass on to me, in your incomparable bounty, your whole will, and kindle within me so great a fire of love that no waters may be able to quench it. O Holy Trinity, my one God and all my good! Ah, would that I could praise and love you as the angels do. If all the love of all created things were mine, how willingly would I hand it over and give it all to you; and yet, not even so would it be a love worthy of you. You alone can worthily love yourself, and worthily praise yourself, for you alone understand your incomprehensible

3. Song 1:15.

bounty, and, thus, you alone can love it as it deserves, and in your most holy breast alone is the just measure of love maintained.

O Mary, Mary, Mary, virgin most holy, mother of God, queen of heaven, sovereign of the world, sanctuary of the Holy Spirit, lily of purity, rose of patience, paradise of delights, mirror of chastity, model of innocence, pray for this poor exile and pilgrim, and give him the crumbs of your most abundant charity.

O all you blessed saints and angels, who burn with the love of your Creator, above all, you Seraphim who set heaven and earth aglow with your love, do not forsake this poor and wretched heart, but purify it—like the lips of Isaiah—from all its sins, and enkindle it with the flame of your most ardent love, that it may love the Lord only, seek him alone, and in him alone for ever and ever rest and dwell. Amen.

12

Certain Counsels to be Followed in this Holy Exercise

ALL THAT WE HAVE SAID SO FAR is meant to provide matter for thought, which is one of the principal things in this business of prayer. Very few, in fact, pay sufficient attention to this, and consequently, through lack of sufficient matter, lose much in this holy exercise.

Now we shall treat briefly of the manner and method we ought to aim at here. Of course the chief master, in this work, is the Holy Spirit; nevertheless, experience has convinced us of the need of certain appropriate counsels, for the path that leads to God is arduous, and, without the necessary guide, many go astray, and lose much time.

FIRST COUNSEL

Here is the first counsel: when we set ourselves to consider any one of the subjects treated of above, at the time fixed and according to the scheme determined on, we should never tie ourselves down so completely as to think it wrong to pass on to some other subject in which we find more devotion, and more benefit. Since the aim is to secure devotion, we should look at what helps us more towards this end as being better. This, however, should not be done lightly, but only where there is a clearly recognized advantage.

Similarly, if at any moment of our prayer or meditation we experience more delight and devotion than at another, we should pause as long as this affection lasts, even though it continue during the whole time of our recollection. As we have said, the purpose throughout is holiness, and it would be a mistake to seek elsewhere, and with doubtful hope of success, what we already hold securely in our hands.

SECOND COUNSEL

The second piece of advice is this: that one should strive to avoid, in this holy exercise, an excessive use of the speculative intellect, endeavouring to treat the matter in hand with the will's affections and sentiments, rather than the intellect's speculative reasoning. Beyond all question, they who meditate in such fashion upon the divine mysteries miss the way, as if they were studying them for preaching purposes. That (mistaken approach) tends to scatter the powers of the soul rather than to recollection, and far from making us enter into ourselves, tends to carry us without. Thus it comes about that, when prayer is over, one is as dry and not devout, and as prompt and ready for every triviality as one was before. To speak truly, such have not prayed at all, but simply composed phrases and studied, which is a very different thing from praying. They should bear in mind that in this exercise we should listen rather than speak.

To succeed in this work, one should undertake it with the heart of an ignorant and humble person, and, better still, with a heart disposed and ready to feel and cling to the things of God, and not with a mind wide awake and attentive to scrutinise them closely. This, indeed, is the characteristic of those who study in order to know, rather than to pray and think about God, in order to weep.

THIRD COUNSEL

The foregoing counsel teaches us how we ought to quiet the understanding and entrust this work to the will. This practice determines for the will its rule and limits, so that it may not act vehemently and without measure. Bear in mind that the devotion we seek cannot be secured—as some fancy—by sheer force. With extreme effort and with a strained and, as it were, fictitious sorrow, some, in thinking of the Savior's passion, manage to produce tears of compassion. But as a rule, this only serves the more to shrivel up the heart and render it unfit for the Savior's coming, as John Cassian teaches.[1]

Besides, this way of acting is very often injurious to health, and sometimes leaves the soul so alarmed at the reaction that follows, as to make it unwilling to undertake again this holy exercise, knowing by experience all the pain there is in it. So let each content himself, in informal fashion, to watch as the Savior suffers, with a quiet and simple gaze, in tenderness and compassion of heart, prepared for whatever

---

1. St. John Cassian, *Conferences,* Part 9, Chapter 29, Abbott Issac on Prayer, www.archive.osb.org/lectio/cassian/conf/book1/conf9.html#9.29.

affections the Master may wish to give him, and ready to suffer for him. He should rather be disposed to receive such affections as his mercy shall give him, than to produce them by his own efforts. This done, let him not be downcast when none are given.

FOURTH COUNSEL

From what has been said we should be able to decipher the kind of attention we ought to have in prayer. The principal thing is that the heart should not be downcast and listless, but vivacious, intent and lifted up. Though it may be necessary to maintain this attention and recollection of heart, it is proper that this attention be restrained and measured, so that it does not injure the health nor impede devotion, for there are indeed some who tax the brain by excessive efforts to be attentive to their thoughts. Others remain listless and inert, and easily liable to be swept away by every wind that blows.

To avoid these extremes, we must pursue a middle course, neither tiring out the mind by excessive attention, nor leaving the mind free to ramble by being so careless and remiss that the mind chases after every thought that comes. Just so, the rider of a restive horse holds the reins firmly—that is, neither too tight nor too slack—so that the animal may not rear backwards on the one hand nor career forward. So we should plan that our attention be moderate and not forced, prompt but not strained and anxious.

We must be very especially warned against wearying the mind, by a too-strained attention at the meditation's start, for our strength is likely to give out for the remainder.

FIFTH COUNSEL

Among all these counsels, a very important one is this: that he who gives himself to prayer should not be troubled, nor abandon this exercise, because he does not at once achieve that sweetness of devotion which he desires.

With long-suffering and patience he must look for the coming of the Lord, his glory, our own lowliness, and the grandeur of the business we have in hand. All conspire to bring it about that often we may be kept waiting, pacing, sentrylike, at the gates of his sacred palace.

If our Lord comes, thank him for his coming; if it seems that he is not coming, humble yourself before him, knowing you do not deserve what is not given you and be content with having made the sacrifice of yourself, renounced your self will, crucified your own natural inclination, struggled with the demon and with yourself, and, at the least, done what you could. If you have not adored our Lord with such fervor of devotion as you would wish, it is enough to have adored him in spirit and in truth, and it is he who would have it thus. Believe me, this is the most challenging place where the really devout are proved. If you come well out of it, all the rest will go well.

Finally, you may think that you are only wasting your time in keeping to this exercise and racking your brains to no purpose. In that case if you have done all you could, no harm comes from taking up some good book and exchanging prayer for reading. The reading, however, must not be quick or hurried, but leisurely and appreciative, mingling prayer with reading. This method is very useful, and well within the reach of even the simplest and most inexperienced.

SIXTH COUNSEL

This counsel is the counterpart of the preceding, and must be given equal prominence. It is this: that the servant of God must not content himself with any part of devotion he may experience in prayer, as some do who, having squeezed out a little tear, or felt some slight kindling of the heart, fancy they have fully accomplished this exercise. The end we are seeking is not secured in this way. Just as a little sprinkling of water merely lays down the dust and damps the surface, it is useless for enriching the soil. But plenty of water is needed to penetrate deep down and spread the fertile moisture there. So we need an abundance of this dew and water from heaven if we are to bring forth the fruit of good works. Hence we are advised, with good reason, to spend over this holy exercise as long a time as we are able, and one period of some length is better than two shorter ones; for where the time is short it is all taken up in controlling the imagination and calming the heart, and barely have we succeeded in doing this, than we finish the exercise at the very moment when we ought to be beginning it.

In determining the length of time for prayer, it seems to me that anything less than an hour and a half or two hours is a short time to assign for prayer.[2] Often enough half an hour is spent in quieting down, as we say, the imagination and bringing the strings of our instrument into tune, and we want all the remainder of the time for relishing the fruit of prayer. It is, of course, true that the heart is better disposed for this work,

2. St. Teresa of Ávila, *Life of . . .* , chapter 7, urged two hours every day. Modern readers would benefit from two periods of prayer each day but the length depends on their generosity as well as time availability.

and, like dry wood, very much more quickly set aglow with the heavenly fire, when this exercise comes after some other holy exercise, like morning prayer, or after one has heard or said Mass, or after some devout reading or vocal prayer. Also, in the morning, the time may be shortened, as one is better disposed then for this work.

However, one who is pressed for time, on account of his many duties, should not cease to offer whatever time he has, like the poor widow in the Temple. For, where there is no negligence, he who provides for all created things according to their needs and nature, will equally also provide for such a one as that.

SEVENTH COUNSEL

In connection with the foregoing counsel, here is another similar one—namely that when the Lord visits a soul, during prayer or outside of it, let it not slip by in vain, but profit by the occasion offered. For it is certain, with such a breeze, that one will sail further in an hour than he otherwise would in many days. It is said of St. Francis that he acted thus. St. Bonaventure relates that his care on this point was such that when our Lord accorded him any special visitation he would, if on a journey, cause his companions to go on ahead, and himself wait behind till he had relished to the full this morsel which had come to him from heaven.[3] Those who do not act in this manner are likely to be punished like this: when they

---

3. St. Bonaventure, *The Life of St. Francis of Assisi,* TAN, Charlotte, NC, chapter 10, part 2.

seek after God, they do not find him, for when he sought after them, they did not seek him in return.

EIGHTH COUNSEL

The last and most important counsel of all is this: that one should endeavour in this holy exercise to mingle meditation with contemplation, making of the one a ladder whereby to mount to the other. To this end we should bear in mind that the work of meditation is to consider, with attentive study, the things of God, now busy on one, now on another, so as to move our hearts to some appropriate sentiments and affections of the will—such as striking a match to secure a flame.

In contemplation, however, the light is already lit—i.e., the sentiment and desired affection of the will is already present. One rests there, and enjoys it in silence, no longer with much intellectual reasoning and speculation, but with undivided attention gazing upon truth. Hence a holy doctor says[4] that meditation reasons with fruit and with toil, contemplation with fruit also, but without toil; the one seeks, the other finds. The one chews on food, the other tastes it; the one turns about from this consideration to that, the other is content with an undistracted view of those things which it already loves and relishes. In a word, one is the means, the other the end; one the path up which we move, the other the end of both path and journey.

---

4. Guigo, *Scala Claustralium*. See archive.org/search.php?query=scalaclaustralium&and[]=subject%3a"Carthusians" (*German edition*).

There follows a well-known truth, taught by all masters of the spiritual life, yet little heeded by those who read—that once the *end* is secured, the *means* are no longer wanted. Just as the sails are reefed when the harbor is reached, so after the work of meditation attains contemplation, one ceases from his work. Content with the single vision and memory of God—as though he saw him present—he should rejoice in such *affections* as are accorded him, of love, or admiration, or delight, or suchlike. The reason for this advice is that the whole purpose of the business lies in love and in the *affections* of the will, rather than in the working of the intellect. So whenever the will is caught up and carried forward by an *affection* of this kind, we ought to set aside, as far as we can, all processes of reasoning and investigation, so that the soul may enter into it as fully as possible, without being disturbed by the action of the other powers.

Hence a wise counsel, that when inflamed with the love of God, one should abandon at once all these thoughts and reflections—however sublime they may seem—not because they are evil in themselves, but because they hinder a greater good. This is nothing else than stopping all movement because we have reached our destination, and giving up meditation for the sake of contemplation. Now this should take place especially at the end of the whole exercise, after the prayer for the love of God. For on the one hand, we may suppose that then the efforts we have made will have given rise to some *affections* and thoughts about God –*Better the end of a thing than its beginning*[5]—and, on the other hand, because,

5. Eccles 7:8.

after the toil of meditation and prayer, it is right to allow one's mind a little repose and to rest in the arms of contemplation.

This is the time to let the products of the imagination slip by unheeded, to quiet down his mental faculties, to calm the working of memory and fix it upon our Lord. Consider oneself as in his presence, without reasoning any further on the attributes of God. Be content with the knowledge of him through faith, and bring into play one's will and love, for with these alone can we cling to God, and in these alone is found the whole fruit of meditation. The understanding is practically powerless to secure a knowledge of God, but the will can achieve much love. Let one be occupied in the center of his soul, where is the image of God. Hearken to him, as one listening to another speaking down to him from a lofty tower, or as though he gazed upon him, present within his own heart, or as though no other thing exists but God and his own soul. Let him be oblivious to himself and his own actions. "Perfect prayer," as one of the Fathers says, "is that during which one who prays is not conscious that he is praying."[6]

We ought to pause awhile and enjoy this favor, not only at the end of the exercise, but also in the middle, or at any other time that this sense of spiritual repose comes over us, in which the understanding is lulled gently to rest by the will. Nor should we return to our exercise till we have relished and digested this morsel. Thus does a gardener act when he is watering a flower bed. After watering it well, he turns off the hose, to allow the water to soak in and penetrate deeply down into the dry soil; then he turns on the

6. St. John Cassian, *Conferences*, part 9, chapter 30. www.archive.osb.org/lectio/cassian/conf/book1/conf9.html#9.30.

hose anew that the soil may receive more and more water, and be more richly refreshed.

In these moments, no words can express what the soul experiences, the light she rejoices in, the fullness and charity and peace she receives. There is the peace that surpasses all understanding and every joy that this life can hold.

Some are so gripped by the love of God that they barely begin to think of him before the memory of his sweet name stirs their innermost being. Such persons have little need of reasoning and considerations to lead them to love him, for they are like the mother or the wife who rejoices at the mere mention of her child or of her husband.

Others are so absorbed and immersed in God during prayer but even outside of it as to be on his account forgetful of all else, and even of themselves. Often enough the wild love of some abandoned wretch can accomplish this; how much more may not the love of this infinite beauty achieve it? Grace, is it less powerful than nature and sin?

When the soul, then, experiences this sentiment, at whatever part of the prayer it may come, let it not, in any way, set this sentiment aside, though the whole time of prayer is passed in that way. Let it engage in no other prayers and meditations unless they be obligatory. For, as St. Augustine says, "One should abandon vocal prayer when it is, in any way, an obstacle to devotion; and similarly one should abandon meditation when it hinders contemplation."[7]

A final, and very important, observation is this: that just as it is fitting to leave meditation for the affections and to

---

7. The Spanish text refers this quotation to the Enchiridion, but I have been unable to identify the passage –Tr.

mount upwards from the lower to the higher, so it is sometimes right to leave the affection and revert to meditation, when the affection is so vehement as to make one fear for one's health if one were to persevere in it. This often happens to those who, ignoring this advice, give themselves to this exercise and, drawn on by the strength of divine sweetness, throw themselves into it without discretion. In such cases, a good remedy is to incline oneself towards an affection of compassion, thinking a little on Christ's passion, or on the world's sins and miseries, so as to ease and alleviate the heart.

Part II

13

The Nature of Devotion

The greatest difficulty from which persons suffer, who give themselves to prayer, is a lack of all devotion; and this is something they often experience. When it does not fail them, there is, of course, nothing sweeter or more easy than prayer. Consequently, having spoken of the matter for prayer and of the method to be employed, it will be a good thing now to treat of those things that foster devotion, and of those that hinder it, of the temptations that most commonly beset devout persons, and finally to give certain practical instructions on this matter.

Before proceeding, however, let's take a moment to make clear what devotion really is. St. Thomas describes it as a virtue which makes one prompt and ready for every good work, which urges him forward and facilitates good deeds.[1] These words show clearly the need and great value of this virtue. There is, indeed, far more in it than many would imagine at first sight.

Remember that the greatest obstacle to leading a good life comes from the corruption of our nature, due to sin. This is

1. St. Thomas Aquinas, *Summa Theologica*, II-II, q. 82, a. 1; and Part I, chapter 1, p. 3–4 of this Treatise. A synonym for "devotion" is "piety."

the cause of that ready inclination we have to what is evil, and of that heaviness and strain which we experience in pursuing what is good. These two hindrances make the path of virtue very difficult for us, though holiness, in itself, is the sweetest and most beautiful thing in the world, and the most worthy of love and honor. To meet this difficulty and sluggish disinclination, divine Wisdom has provided a most fitting remedy in the virtue and support of devotion.

Just as the north wind scatters the clouds and leaves a clear and open sky, so does true devotion brush away from the soul this difficulty, and leave it agile and unencumbered, ready for every good work. This virtue is not, indeed, of any ordinary kind, for it is also a special gift of the Holy Spirit, a dew from heaven, a support sent by God. It is won through prayer. It helps in a number of ways: to banish lukewarmness and fill its place with promptness, to fill the soul with high purposes, to enlighten the intellect and fortify the will, to enkindle the fire of divine love and extinguish the flames of evil desire, to impart a distaste of the world and a horror of sin, and to establish a new fervor, a new spirit, and new strength and determination in well-doing. As long as the locks on Samson's head remained untouched, he was stronger than any other man, but once they were cut, he became as weak as the rest. So is devotion for the Christian soul; deprived of it, and it weakens at once.

What St. Thomas wishes us to understand from his definition, and it is the greatest praise one can bestow is that devotion stands alone as stimulus and incentive for every other virtue. Consequently he who really wishes to advance along the path of holiness should never set out without trying to live this virtue, in order to overcome the difficulties he will encounter.

From what we have said, the true and essential characteristic of devotion may be clearly grasped. Not in any mere tenderness of heart does it lie, nor in that consolation which those who pray are likely at times to experience, unless these be accompanied by a readiness and zeal to act well. It often happens that when our Lord would test his own, the one is present without the other.

This devotion and alacrity frequently lead to consolation, and, conversely, this same consolation and delight in spiritual things increase that real devotion which lies in a promptness and zeal for doing good. For this reason the servants of God may long and pray for these consoling joys, not for any delight they give, but because they serve to strengthen that devotion which facilitates good actions. Such is the sense of those words of the prophet: *I will run in the way of thy commandments, when thou enlarge my understanding!*[2]

Finally, we shall explain the means for acquiring devotion; and since this virtue is knit with all those which bind us in any way intimately with God, it will mean examining the ways for acquiring perfect prayer and contemplation, as well as the consolations of the Holy Spirit, the love of God, divine wisdom and that union of our souls with God which is the whole purpose of a spiritual life. Last of all we shall study how we may in this life win possession of God himself. This is the treasure of which the Gospel speaks, that pearl of great price, for which the wise merchant sells cheerfully all that he owns.

2. Ps 119 (118):32.

Thus we are embark upon a very lofty theology, since it teaches us the way to the sovereign good, and, step by step, extends the ladder whence we may grasp the fruit of happiness insofar as is possible in this life.

14

Nine Aids to Devotion

MANY THINGS CONTRIBUTE to devotion. First, it is very important to enter seriously and steadfastly upon these holy exercises, and with a very resolute heart, ready for whatever may be necessary, however difficult to secure this pearl of great price. Certainly, nothing great comes without difficulty. *Ad astra per aspera.* So it is in this case, at least for beginners.

Keep guard also over the heart, banishing every kind of vain and idle thought, all alien emotions of love, all passionate and tempestuous movement. Clearly enough these all impede devotion. Like the viola, would we play on it, so also the heart, if would we pray and meditate, must be kept well-modulated.

Keep watch also over the senses, especially the eyes, the ears and the tongue, for through the lips is the heart scattered, and by eyes and ears is it filled with various imaginings, and with much that disturbs the soul's peace and repose. For the less it dissipates its energies outside, the more will it be recollected within. The contemplative soul *should be deaf, dumb and blind, quite indifferent in fact, to everything in which spiritual profit is not found.*[1]

1. St. Bonaventure, Treatise *De XXV Memorialibus. #24.* See *A Franciscan View of the Spiritual and Religious Life,* Dominic Deval, London 1922, p. 145. (online text) https://ia800206.us.archive.org/20/items/franciscanviewof00bonauoft/franciscanviewof00bonauoft.pdf.

For the same reason, one should incline towards a solitary life, for not merely does it remove from the senses occasions of distraction, and from the heart occasions of sin, but it also invites one to enter more into the interior life, and to occupy oneself alone with God. For to God one is much drawn by circumstances of place, when no alien company there finds admittance.

Then, make a practice of reading spiritual and devout books. They serve to feed the imagination and to keep the heart recollected, and they lead those of good will to occupy their mind. For what fills the heart first suggests itself to the mind. Keep the thought of God continually before you, and walk always in his presence. Make use of those short prayers which St. Augustine calls *aspirations*—they guard the mansion of the heart and maintain, as we have said above, the warmth of devotion. Be ready at any moment to give yourself to prayer. This is one of the most essential principles of a spiritual life, and among the best resources for such as have neither time nor opportunity for fixed prayer; and anyone who bears this counsel in mind and puts it into practice will make great progress in quite a short time.

Add to this, continuity and perseverance in these holy exercises, at the time and place fixed, especially night and morning, which, as all Holy Scripture teaches us, are the most suitable for prayer. Practice some austerity and bodily abstinence, a poor diet, a hard bed, hair-shirt and discipline, and such-like. These things result from devotion and also contribute to it, preserving and strengthening the root from which they spring.[2]

2. St. Ignatius, *The Spiritual Exercises: Addition,* 10, p. 32–33, www.documentacatholica.eu/03d/1491-1556,_Ignatius_Loyola,_Spiritual_Exercises,_En.pdf.

Lastly, practice works of mercy. In our own sufferings they give us confidence before God; they contribute much to the value of our prayers, which can no longer be called mere arid petitions, and they secure for them a reception full of mercy, seeing that they proceed from a merciful heart.

15

Ten Hindrances to Devotion

JUST AS CERTAIN things help devotion, others impede it. Among the latter sin is the first, and not merely mortal sin, but venial sins also, for these, although they do not deprive us of charity, diminish its fervor, which is practically the same thing as devotion. Consequently we should be very much on our guard against them, not so much for the evil they work in us, as for the great good of which they despoil us.

A second hindrance is the remorse of conscience—when it is excessive—which proceeds from these sins, for it disturbs and casts down the soul, frightens it and makes it unfit for every good work.

Scruples, for the same reason, constitute another hindrance. They are like thorns, allowing the soul no rest, so that it can neither repose in God nor enjoy true peace.

Every kind of bitterness, sadness and unreasoning depression are also hindrances, for one can hardly find satisfaction in a good conscience and in spiritual joy.

Overmuch worry is a further hindrance. Cares are like the flies of Egypt[1] which distress the soul and prevent it from enjoying that spiritual rest which is experienced in prayer. It

1. Ex 8:24.

is precisely then, more than at other times, that they disturb the soul and turn it away from this exercise.

Too many occupations are also a hindrance, for they take up a lot of time, stifle the soul, and leave a man without leisure or heart for divine things. Pleasure and worldly consolations, if indulged to excess, hinder a man from prayer.

Delicacy and abundance in food and drink form another hindrance, and especially long-drawn-out repasts. These are a very bad foundation for spiritual exercises and devout perseverance in prayer. When the body is weighed down and charged in excess with food, the soul is very unfitted to soar aloft.[2]

The vice of curiosity in the senses and in the intellect is also a hindrance. Seeking to hear and see all sorts of things, wishing to have about one things that are pretty or quaint or wonderfully worked, all this takes up time, overstimulates the senses, disturbs the soul and diverts it in every direction, and thus impedes devotion.

Finally, any interruption of these holy exercises, unless for a good and pious reason, since the spirit of devotion is something very delicate, and once it goes, it either does not return at all, or, at least, only after much difficulty. As a tree needs water, and the human body its regular nourishment, in default of which they wither and weaken and die, so it is with devotion, when the waters of consideration and its nourishing force are withdrawn from it.

All this has been said very hastily, that the memory may be better able to retain it. Its truth will become apparent to anyone who is willing to make a good attempt at these exercises.

---

2. St. Bernard, *Sermons on Advent and Christmas*, pp. 130–131, https://archive.org/details/sermonsofstberna00bernuoft/page/130/mode/2up.

16

The Temptations which Usually Beset Those Who Give Themselves to Prayer, and their Remedies

NOW LET US TURN to the more usual temptations met with by persons who give themselves to prayer, and to their remedies. They are usually as follows: the absence of spiritual consolation; the struggle with annoying thoughts; thoughts against faith, and of blasphemy; excessive fear; an immoderate tendency to sleep; timidity or overconfidence about one's spiritual progress; presumptuous estimate of one's progress; an inordinate desire of knowledge; and an indiscreet zeal to attain perfection. Such are the more common temptations that beset this path.

The following are the remedies:

FIRST COUNSEL

For those who lack spiritual consolation the remedy is as follows: do not, on this account, abandon the customary exercise of prayer, though it appear insipid to you, and of little fruit, but rather prostrate yourself in the presence of God as a guilty sinner.

Examine your conscience and see if, perhaps, it may not be through some fault of your own that you have lost this grace. Offer your supplications to our Lord with a complete confidence of pardon, and extol the inestimable riches of his patience and of his mercy.

In this way a man will draw profit from his aridity, taking occasion to humiliate himself the more at the sight of all his sins, and to love God more in beholding the vastness of his pardon. Though there be no enjoyment in all this, let him not give up, for what is profitable is not necessarily always agreeable; and experience, at least, shows that every effort to persevere in prayer brings consolation and joy. He does much, in the eyes of God, who does all he can, though it be but little.

Our Lord does not consider so much one's capabilities as one's good will in doing all that is possible for him. He gives much who longs to give much, and does actually give his all. It is no great thing to spend much time in prayer, when consolations abound. However, long prayer—when devotion is slight—and a growing humility and patience and perseverance in the good is indeed much.

On these occasions it is also necessary to be more on one's guard than at other times, and more careful, keeping diligent watch over oneself, and with much attention examining one's thoughts, words and actions. Since we lack that spiritual delight which is our main oar in this voyage, we must make up by care and diligence for our deficiency in grace.

"When you come to such a pass as this," says St. Bernard, "you must realize once for all that the watchmen who guarded you are wrapped in sleep, and that your sheltering walls have fallen. Your one remaining hope of safety is in your own arms. A wall is your defence no longer, but your sword and your skill in the fight. Oh, how great is the glory of a soul which combats in this manner, defending herself without shield, fighting though unarmed, strong though defenceless, struggling alone in the conflict, with nought to bear her company but her own audacity and courage."[1]

In this world, no greater glory exists than to imitate the virtues of our Savior. Chief among these virtues is to have suffered as he did, without consolation; and thus he who suffers also and struggles will be all the truer an imitator of Christ in proportion as he too lacks all manner of consolation. This is, indeed, to drink the pure chalice of obedience, unsweetened by anything else. This is the touchstone showing where the refinement of friendship is to be found, and marking off the true friends from those who are not.

SECOND COUNSEL

Against the temptation of annoying thoughts, which quite commonly assail us in prayer, the remedy lies in combating them manfully and perseveringly. This effort, however, should never be carried to the point of excessive fatigue and distress of soul, for it is really less an affair of energy than of grace and humility. When this condition arises, one should turn towards God without any scruple or misgiving, for, in all

1. *Epistola: Ad Fratres de Monte Dei,* attributed to St. Bernard, but rather to be ascribed to Guigo the Carthusian.

this, there is no fault on his part, or but a very slight one. With entire devotion and humility say: "See, Lord, what I am: what can you expect from such refuse but odors of this kind? What can you look for from the earth which you have cursed but brambles and thorns? This is the only fruit she can bear you, if you cleanse her not."

When this is done, take up again the thread of your prayer as before and with patience wait for the visit of our Lord, who never fails those who are humble. Should these same thoughts still assail you, know for certain that if you persevere in your resistance and do your best, you will gain far more ground than by dwelling in the enjoyment of God amid every delight.

THIRD COUNSEL

The remedy for temptations to blasphemy is to realize that no sort of temptation is more distressing than this, and none less dangerous. The cure is not to make much of these temptations. To experience them is no sin; sin lies in consenting and delighting in them; and there is nothing of that here, but rather the contrary. Consequently they must be regarded as a punishment rather than a fault.

The absence of any pleasure derived from them must be taken as the measure of our blamelessness. Hence, as I say, the remedy is to ignore these temptations, and not to be afraid of them. When one is very much afraid of them, this dread itself awakens them and brings them on.

FOURTH COUNSEL

Against temptations to infidelity the remedy is to reflect on the littleness of human nature on the one hand, and on the greatness of God on the other. Think of the commandments of God without being obsessed over your own actions, since much that we see altogether exceeds our understanding. As for one who would enter into this sanctuary of the works of God, let him approach with great humility and reverence, and lift up the simple eyes of the dove, not those of a malevolent serpent, and let his heart be as that of a disciple and not as that of one ready rashly to judge. Let him become as a little child, for to such does God declare his secrets. Let him not strive to know the *reason* for the works of God; let him close the eye of his understanding and open that of his faith, for this is the instrument with which to examine the works of God. For studying the works of man, this eye of human reason is excellent; but for seeing those that are divine, there is nothing more completely unfit.

As this temptation is also likely to be most trying, like the preceding one of annoying thoughts, so is the remedy the same—viz., to make light of it. It is a trial rather than a fault. There can be no fault where the will opposes that fault.

FIFTH COUNSEL

Some people, when they set themselves to pray alone and by night, are harassed by terrifying imaginations. The remedy for this temptation is to mortify oneself, and to persevere. Our fear increases if we fly from it, while our courage grows stronger as we resist. It is well to reflect also that neither the devil nor any power at all can contrive anything to our hurt without our Lord's permission. It is also useful to remember that we have by our side our guardian angel, and that he is even nearer to us in prayer than at other times, for then he stands by to help us and to bear our prayers heavenwards and to shield us from the enemy, who is thus powerless to do us any hurt.

SIXTH COUNSEL

Against an excessive tendency to sleep, the remedy is to bear in mind that this is sometimes caused by sheer necessity, in which case the thing to do is not to deny the body what is due to it, that the body itself may not hinder what is due to the soul.

At other times it comes from ill health, in which case no one should be disturbed, since there is no fault here. Yet neither should one allow oneself to be wholly vanquished, without quietly doing what one can, so as not entirely to lose hold of prayer, without which there is no security nor true joy in this life. Lastly, this tendency to sleep comes sometimes from idleness or from the devil inclining us to it. Here the remedy lies in fasting, drinking no wine, and but little water, keeping oneself on one's knees, or standing, or with arms extended, without support, in taking the discipline or in performing other acts of austerity which prick and stir up the body.[2]

---

2. St. Ignatius, *The Spiritual Exercises, Addition,* 10, www.documentacatholica.eu/03d/1491-1556,_Ignatius_Loyola,_Spiritual_Exercises,_En.pdf.

Finally, a single and comprehensive remedy, as well for this as for all other evils, is to ask relief from him who is ever ready to give to those who know how to ask perseveringly.

SEVENTH COUNSEL

As for temptations to fearfulness and to presumption, these being contrary vices, different remedies must naturally be applied. For fearfulness or timidity, the remedy is to consider that success is not to be achieved by personal efforts alone, but by the grace of God, which is secured all the more promptly in proportion as a man is distrustful of his own strength and confident only in the goodness of God, to whom all is possible.

For presumption, the remedy lies in remembering that there is no surer sign of being far away than fancying one is near. For on this journey those who cover the more ground are quicker to see how very much is still lacking in them. Hence they make little of what they possess when they compare it to what they seek. Use the lives of the saints, and of other holy persons still living, as you would a mirror. Consider that compared to them, you are a dwarf before a giant, and your presumption disappears.

EIGHTH COUNSEL

Against the temptation which consists in an immoderate desire to study and to know, the first remedy is to consider how far more excellent holiness is than learning, and divine wisdom than what is human; and this should lead you to busily acquire the one rather than the other.

Think of the wisdom of this world, its glory and the grandeur of its aims; yet at the end, like life itself, this glory also vanishes. What more wretched than to win with so much effort what one can but so briefly enjoy? However far-reaching your knowledge, it yet is as nothing; but if you exercise yourself in the love of God, quickly will you come to see him, and, seeing him, to see all. "At the day of judgement we shall not be asked what we have read, but what we have done; not how successfully we have spoken or preached, but how well we have labored."[3]

NINTH COUNSEL

The remedy for indiscreet zeal in working for others' good is to apply ourselves to our neighbor's help without harming our own welfare.

Thus we should devote ourselves to matters of conscience of others in such a way as to have time also for our own. This time should be sufficiently long to enable us to maintain our hearts always in devout recollection.

This, as the apostle Paul says, is *to walk by the spirit,*[4] when, that is, a man lives more in God than in himself. Since here lies the root and principle of all our good, our whole endeavour should be to maintain a spirit of prayer, at once so wide and deep, as will serve to keep our hearts always recollected and devout. For this not just any kind of prayer and recollection suffices, but we need what is very penetrating and very intense.

3. Thomas à Kempis, *The Imitation of Christ,* Bk 1, ch. 3.

4. Gal 5:16.

17

Certain Counsels Necessary for Those Who Give Themselves to Prayer

IN THIS LIFE IT IS DIFFICULT to know how to turn to God and to deal naturally with him. There is no advancing along this road without a good guide whose warnings may prevent straying off it. Some of these warnings will be necessary to take note of here.

FIRST COUNSEL

The first counsel concerns the end we ought to propose to ourselves in these exercises. We should note that dealing with God is, as the Psalm says,[1] something very delightful and agreeable. It comes about, then, that many persons, gripped by this sweetness which surpasses all power of description, attach themselves to God and devote themselves to spiritual exercise, reading, prayer, and frequent reception of the sacraments, precisely on account of the great delight they obtain.

1. Ps 31(30):20.

Here, indeed, is a great and very widespread error into which many fall. The principal end of all our works should be to love God and to seek after God; whereas these are much rather loving themselves and seeking after themselves. One's own happiness and contentment is the end philosophers propose to themselves in their speculations. "This," says Henricus Harphius, "is a species of avarice, of luxury and spiritual greed, and it is no less perilous than what is sensual."[2]

Even worse is that from this error another, no less evil, arises: to judge oneself and others according to these feelings of devotional delight, fancying that each one has more or less of perfection according as he enjoys it in a greater or lesser degree. This is a complete mistake.

Against these two errors of delight in devotion and judgement cast on others by this measure, here is a piece of advice of general application: let each grasp once for all that the end of all these exercises and of the whole spiritual life is simply obedience to the commandments of God and the accomplishment of the divine will. To achieve this we must die to our own will, that the will of God, which is in opposition to it, may live and reign.

So great a victory is not to be won without great favors and kindness on God's part. Consequently we must devote ourselves to the exercise of prayer so as to secure these favors and to experience this kindness, and thus to succeed in our enterprise. From this point of view and with this purpose before us, it is legitimate, as we have said above, to pray for and procure a delight in prayer.

---

2. Henricus Harphius, *Theologia Mystica*, book 3, chapter 26.

David did so when he said: *Restore to me the joy of your salvation, and uphold me with a willing spirit.*[3] When one grasps the end he ought to propose to himself in these exercises, he will understand how to judge and measure his own progress and that of others, not by the delight he may have received from God, but by what he has endured for his sake, in doing God's will and setting aside his own.

That this is indeed the purpose of all our spiritual reading and prayer needs no further proof than that provided by the divine prayer or Psalm 118 known as the *Beati immaculati in via*. This psalm has one hundred and seventy-six verses—it is the longest in the Psalter—and not one verse that does not make mention of the will of God and the keeping of his commandments. The Holy Spirit has wished it to be so, that all might learn how every prayer and meditation, both wholly and in part, should be directed towards this end, namely, obedience, and the keeping of the law of God. To stray from this is to fall into one of the enemy's most subtly veiled artifices, where he leads men to think something of themselves, whereas they are nothing.

Very wisely, then, do the saints tell us that the true touchstone for a man is not the delight he may experience in prayer, but his patience in tribulation, self-abnegation and doing of the will of God, to which, of course, spiritual consolations may themselves undoubtedly contribute.

In conformity with this principle, he who would measure his advance in this path of God, should ask himself how much each day he has progressed in exterior and interior humility.

---

3. Ps 51 (50):12.

How does he take insults from another? How ready is he to pardon the weaknesses of others? How prompt is he to come to his neighbor's needs? Is he filled with compassion or with indignation at others' faults? Does he know how to trust God in times of adversity? How does he control his tongue? How does he guard his affections? Does he keep his body in subjection, and all its cravings, and his senses? To what extent does he know how to draw profit from prosperity and from adversity? How does he control himself, and what is his manner in all the circumstances of life? Is it characterized by gravity and discretion? Above all, mark how far he is dead to the love of honor, of pleasure, and of the world.

It is in such ways as these, advancing or falling back, that a man should judge himself; and not by what he feels or does not feel in prayer. Consequently he must have one eye busy always taking stock of his mortification—which is the more important side—and the other taking stock of his prayer, for without the help of prayer, mortification itself cannot be perfectly secured.

SECOND COUNSEL

If we should not wish for consolations and spiritual delights merely in order to bask in them, but simply to profit from them, much less should anyone desire visions, revelations, ecstasies and so forth, which may be very dangerous to such as are not founded in humility.

Let no one fear going against the will of God here. When God wishes to reveal anything, he knows the means of doing so. The more one hides himself, the more does God reveal his word, so much so that even if one wanted to, one could not doubt.

THIRD COUNSEL

Similarly we must be warned to hide the favors and gifts our Lord bestows upon us, except only from our spiritual father. It is this which makes St. Bernard say that a man ought to have these words written on the walls of his room: "My secret to myself, my secret to myself."[4]

FOURTH COUNSEL

Deal with God with very great humility and the deepest possible respect. However much a soul may be enriched and favor by God, it should never cease to turn its eyes inwards upon itself, to consider its unworthiness, to fold its wings and humble itself before such great majesty. So did St. Augustine act, who learned to rejoice with fear in the presence of God.

FIFTH COUNSEL

Each ought to set aside a fixed time in which to devote himself to prayer. In addition to this ordinary and daily exercise, he should at times withdraw himself completely from every kind of occupation, however holy it may be, so as to concentrate upon spiritual exercises and give abundant nourishment to his soul.

---

4. St. Bernard, *Sermon XXIII super Cantica*: Is 24:16.

Thus the loss occasioned by daily faults may be repaired, and new strength acquired for further progress. This may be done at any time, but especially at the times of the principal feasts of the year, and in periods of trouble and distress, or after a long journey or any absorbing business which may have led to distraction and dissipation of heart, in order to reestablish it in recollection.

SIXTH COUNSEL

Some, when all passes smoothly in their exercises of devotion towards God, show themselves lacking in due discretion. For them prosperity itself becomes an occasion of danger. Grace seems to many to descend upon them in overflowing measure: so sweet do they find their dealing with our Lord. So completely do they throw themselves into it, increasing their times of prayer, their vigils and their physical austerities, that nature can no longer support this continuous burden, and together they fall to the ground.

Often, a reaction then sets in. They starve themselves, thus becoming unfit not only for bodily work, but even for prayer itself.

Thus a great deal of circumspection is required, especially at the beginning—when fervor and consolations are great, and experience and discretion very slight—in order that we may set out upon this journey as not to collapse half way.

The opposite extreme, that of the self-indulgent, will under color of discretion, avoid all physical exertion. This is dangerous for everybody, but especially for beginners. As St. Bernard says, "He cannot possibly persevere in the religious life who, as a novice, is already full of discretion,"[5] that is, as a beginner, is overcautious, and, while still young, looks after his health as carefully as an old man.

It is not easy to say which of these two extremes is the more perilous, except that indiscretion is the harder to cure.

SEVENTH COUNSEL

Among the perils is yet another, and one, perhaps, greater than any of the preceding. Many persons, having experienced the inestimable value of prayer, and seen for themselves how the whole framework of a spiritual life depends upon it, come to imagine that prayer alone is everything, that alone it is sufficient to secure their salvation. They begin, in consequence, to forget about the other virtues, and to grow widely indifferent. Thus it comes about that, as all the virtues contribute to prayer, once the foundation weakens, the whole edifice falls; and the more a man strives to rebuild it, the less he is able to succeed.

Thus one must not fix his attention exclusively on one virtue, however great, but upon them all. Just as, in a viola, one string alone cannot produce harmonious music unless the others are made to contribute, so any single virtue is not sufficient to secure this spiritual harmony unless the others join in unison. A single defect destroys the whole value of a clock; so also is it with a spiritual life if but one virtue falters.

---

5. St. Bernard, *Epistola ad Fratres de Monte Dei* (Sic et animalem discretum novitium prudentem, incipientem sapieutem in cella diu posse consistere, in congregatione durare, impossibile est." (PL 184, 317D) Attributed to William of St. Thierry, although often ascribed to St. Bernard. https://openlibrary.org/books/OL22029122M/Die_Epistola_ad_fratres_de_Monte_Dei.

EIGHTH COUNSEL

And now we must point out that everything we have suggested so far as aiding devotion, is simply of the nature of a preparation to dispose oneself for divine grace with all diligence, and yet not trust such means as these, but solely in God.

I say this, because some people are likely to make a regular system out of all these rules and counsels. They fancy that, just as in learning a trade, he who carefully follows the established rules will soon become quite proficient in consequence, so also here, they imagine that if they duly follow these prescribed regulations, they will quickly secure what they desire. They fail to see that this is to put grace on the same level as an art, and to attribute to rules and human devices what is a gift of God's mercy.

Viewing it thus, one can see that the principal means to use are a deep humility, flowing from a recognition of one's own misery, and a very great confidence in divine mercy. From this double source unceasing tears and prayers always flow. With these, entering by the gate of humility, a man obtains by humility what he is seeking, with humility he preserves it, and with humility he rejoices in it, placing no confidence either in himself or in the method of his exercises.

Part III

18

A Brief Instruction for Those Who Are Beginning to Serve Our Lord[1]

As every human art has its elementary principles which form, as it were, the ABC by which one begins, so is it also with this progress towards God, which is the art of arts and the whole purpose of life. It will be a good thing, then, to point out these principles briefly, for the benefit of those who wish to enter upon it.

The first steps in anything are always comparatively easy, so it will be wise to begin by indicating those spiritual exercises which present but little difficulty, and are as the milk in this process of spiritual nourishment. Just as fish can only live in water, so an interior life can only be maintained by means of spiritual exercises.

To begin with, a man must first make up his mind to serve God and to abandon a worldly life, and, for this purpose, make a general confession of all the sins of his past life. With this end in view, he should set aside a few days in order

1. *This Brief Instruction*, and the *Three Things*, are found in the Lisbon. edition of *The Treatise on Prayer and Meditation*, c. 1558.

to go back over the various stages of his past life, recalling all the commandments of the divine law, and, with sorrow and bitterness of heart, examining all he has said, done or thought against God, his neighbour and himself. He should then go to confession to his own proper confessor, putting pen to paper, if need be, in order to assist the weakness of memory. And here a good spiritual director should teach his penitent how to examine his conscience and prepare himself and make his confession, both the general confession and the ordinary ones, which ought to be more detailed. It is not easy to get to know oneself and make a fruitful confession, except with advice and guidance.

The second step is to apply oneself to the meditations outlined above, especially to those of the first week—which are better adapted for this stage—disposing the heart, by their means, to sorrow and a detestation of sin, to the fear of God and contempt for the world. This is the most opportune moment for the director to explain the method of prayer and meditation, and to develop all the suggestions indicated already. He should be very precise in providing nourishment and should know how to instruct well, that from the hands of a competent director the disciple may come forth thoroughly instructed.

The third lies in instructing the disciple as to the great respect and devotion with which he should prepare himself, a day or so beforehand, for Holy Communion, with what fear and trembling he ought to approach, with what devotion he should recollect himself in order to embrace the Lord he is receiving, casting himself at his feet and thanking him for such a visit and for so great a favor. He should understand, also, how recollected and calm he should be that day, and the day preceding, and in what sort of reading, meditation and prayer he should prepare.

The fourth is to teach the manner in which a man should bear himself at all places and times, and in all his exterior occupations; with what sobriety and suitability he should take his meals at table; what devotion and respect he should have when assisting at Mass, and when receiving Communion; how, with reverent attention, he should assist at the divine offices, preparing himself beforehand by prayer and recollection of heart, and, while they are in progress, striving energetically to banish every nagging fantasy of the imagination with which the enemy then, more than at any other time, assails us.

Instruct the newcomer, also, how to be restrained in all his movements, watchful over his eyes, measured in his words, restrained in his laughter, humble before his superiors, kindly with those below him, courteous towards his equals, full of sympathy with the poor, compassionate towards the infirm, and in nothing whatsoever either hasty or inconsiderate.

Teach him, moreover, how to walk in the presence of God, having him ever before his eyes as judge and witness of his life, so that he gives as much time and devout attention to every duty as he would if he saw God actually present before him.

Then instruct him as to how to live always enclosed and hidden within his heart, and how at all times and places, and in every kind of business, he should steal his mind away and lift it up to God by a little prayer, using everything he sees or hears as an occasion for so doing, like the bees who from every flower take at least something to make honey.

It is a very praiseworthy custom, following the example of St. Bartholomew, to kneel down often by day and by night, or even to stand upright or in any other posture, and to pray to God, joining one's hands and offering oneself to our Lord with all one's desires, and begging of him his love and his grace, even though the whole takes no longer than one Creed or two. Many a time, from a devout practice like this, more profit is derived than one can imagine. It serves to keep alive the fire on the altar, feeding it with all these considerations and devout prayers which are as the sustenance of devotion and of the love of God.

Should the mind wander away at times, it should be gathered again and brought back within, but without any of that anxious effort which is so common; rather with love and devotion. For, as the saints tell us, all these negligences fade to nothing and are consumed in the fire of divine love. Then may one, turning towards oneself, gently blame oneself, saying: "Where have I been, O good Jesus: how comes it that I have drawn apart from you? Where have you flown to, my soul? And what have you won but distractions and tepidity? Don't you know that our Lord is with those who live recollected, and that he draws away from those who draw away from the seclusion of their own hearts?"

At all times be as recollected as possible, but particularly on waking in the morning one should try to close the door to every kind of worldly thought, filling the mansion of his mind with the memory of our Lord, and straightaway offering to him the first fruits of the day. Three things he may then proceed to do: *Firstly,* to give thanks for the gift of a quiet night, untroubled by the fantasies and ambushes of the enemy, and then for all such other benefits as creation, preservation, vocation, redemption, etc. *Secondly,* to offer up all the actions, sufferings and labors of the coming day, all the various undertakings and duties in which one will be busy during it, and finally to offer up oneself also, with all that one has, that all may be to the glory of God, and that he may throughout dispose of all, as of what is rightly his own, according to his holy will. *Thirdly,* to beg grace to do nothing, that day, that may offend his Majesty, and especially to beg this favor against those vices to which we are most tempted, arming ourselves against them by a strong determination and by watchfulness. Then recite a *Hail Mary* slowly and devoutly.

In the evening, before going to bed, one should examine their conscience and take account of all they have done that day, or said, or thought against the law of God, and of the neglect and tepidity shown in his service, and one's forgetfulness of him. One should say the *Confiteor* with devotion, and an *Our Father* and a *Hail Mary.* Then one may ask pardon for the evil they have done, and for the grace to make amends.

In bed, he should settle himself as though he were in his tomb, thinking for a moment what his body would look like then, say to himself, as if to a dead person, a *response,* or an *Our Father* and *Hail Mary*. As often as he wakes during the night he should say a *Glory be . . . ,* or *Jesus our redeemer . . .* or any similar prayer. Each time he hears the clock strike the hour, he should say: "Blessed be the hour in which my Lord Jesus Christ was born, and died for me. Lord, at the hour of my death, remember me." Then he should think how he has an hour less of life, and that, little by little, his voyage is drawing to a close.

When one is at table, they may think how it is God who gives them to eat and that he has made all things to serve him. He should thank him for the food he provides, and reflect on those who lack that in which he abounds, and how easily there comes to him what others can only secure with so much work and peril.

When one is tempted by the enemy, the best remedy is to hasten with all speed to the Cross, and to see Christ there, covered with wounds, torn, disfigured, streaming with blood. Then one should reflect that the chief reason why he is there is to destroy sin; and so, with all devotion, beg him not to allow what is so abominable, and what he sought, with such work, to overthrow, ever to reign in his heart.

Then he may say to him lovingly: "Lord, you brought yourself to this, that I might not sin, and yet, after all, it is not sufficient to keep me away from sin! By those most sacred wounds, allow it not, O Lord! O my God, do not forsake me; it is to you I come, for I see no safer refuge where I may be healed. If you forsake me, what will become of me, where shall I turn to, who will defend me? Help me, O Lord, my God, and preserve me. Without you I can do nothing."

It is an excellent practice often to make the sign of the Cross, if it can be done without being noticed. Thus temptations will be an occasion for him to raise up his heart to God often during the day, and win a more glorious crown. As for the devil, who came, as the saying is, *for the wool,* he goes back shorn himself.

Such, Christian reader, is the milk for beginners. Now, in what follows, comes a summary of all this spiritual doctrine.

19

Three Practices to Advance Quickly

He who, by the grace of our Lord, wishes to profit much in a short time should be solicitous about three things.

The first is austerity and mortification of the flesh; roughness, asperity and temperance in eating and drinking, in one's clothing, bed and suchlike; praying on one's knees, or standing erect, prostrate or with arms extended; taking the discipline, wearing a hairshirt, fasting, and, above all, watching devoutly in prayer; prompt to profit by occasions of afflicting the body and banishing self-love, without, however, injuring one's health. For this the advice of one's director should be sought, or, if none, then of any other person known to be spiritual, mortified and exemplary.

Very few understand a holy life except in so far as they practice it. Should this exterior aid be lacking, help yourself with as much discretion as you may, relying upon our Lord and not on the prudence of the flesh. One whom God favors must begin with discretion, testing here and there in turn; but experience, prayer and a pure intention end by making clear what is to be done.

Second and more important is this: to be intent upon one's own interior mortification, desires and sensual inclinations, upon the giving up of one's own will in order to accomplish God's will and that of superiors to whom one owes obedience, and of one's director, if one has one. Then be intent upon the exercise of virtue, interior and exterior, as occasion may demand, or the obligation of charity which we owe, or, finally, as our Lord may interiorly invite us to, without, however, placing us under any obligation.

Third is to be intent unceasingly upon prayer, for it is impossible to crucify the flesh. And, even more impossible for us is interior mortification, self-renunciation, and the practice of virtues, which are beyond nature, without the help of our Lord's grace. For him, it is very easy to work within us upon our whole nature, and he will do it instantly if we ask it of him. We are poor and have no energy for toil, but if we would be rich with the gifts of heaven, we must beg them from him who will never cease bestowing them upon us, if we, on our side, cease not to implore them. He who would enrich himself with these gifts and above all, would, by a special grace, possess God, should have his determined times of prayer, which, as has been said, he should occasionally prolong, and he should walk always in the presence of our Lord, as we have explained.

These three principal practices should be lived to make one's sacrifice pure and perfect. By maintaining these three points, a person is entirely reformed in all ways—both in soul, mind and body. By fasts and corporal austerities is the body sanctified; by the mortifications and abnegation of all its inclinations the mind is sanctified; while by prayer and contemplation the soul advances towards that ultimate perfection in which, by uniting it to God, it becomes one with him.

But here we should note that, for the completion of this sacrifice, two things are needed, for the body has its senses, and the mind its imagination and its thoughts. Consequently, to the three points mentioned above we must add two more—to guard one's senses, the eyes, the ears and, above all, the tongue, which is the key of all; and secondly, to guard one's heart or imagination, that it not be free to roam at will, running hither and thither as it chooses, but may dwell always in holy considerations and thoughts. "It is not enough," says St. Bernard, "for a devout man to curb his affections, if he does not also restrain his imagination and keep it recollected."[1]

In summary, the heart of man, free from sin, needs help if it is to work well, as the earth does if it is to bear fruit. For the soil requires rain and dew from the heavens, and man's cultivation here below. Without these, the earth of itself can produce only briars and thorns. So also must we see that, as a result of sin, our heart of itself can bring forth only those thorns of which St. Paul speaks: *Now the works of the flesh are plain: immorality, impurity, licentiousness. . . .*[2]

If we would secure the fruit of eternal life, we must work in the sweat of our brow, and with the water and dew of heaven. In the sweat of our brow we must practice mortification of the flesh, custody of the senses, control of concupiscence, and watchfulness over the imagination. It is the spiritual effort corresponding to the cultivation of the soil.

---

1. St. Bernard, *De Deo orando.*

2. Gal 5:19.

For the latter we have the sacraments and prayer. The sacraments serve to secure for us this water from heaven, which is grace; and the work of prayer is to beg for this, and then to obtain it as a recompense. Thus, by the intervention of God's grace and man's work, this earth of malediction brings forth the fruit of benediction, provided always that our own toil is not itself devoid of grace, for from God alone every good thing must come.

Thus—to sum up—the life of every true and perfect Christian must be a mingling of unceasing prayer and work; two feet are essential for us on this journey: the one work, the other prayer. Let a man trust himself to God and toil with constancy for his love; but not, on the one hand, by a foolish confidence in God, to allow himself to slumber, nor, on the other, by excessive reliance on his own efforts, to come to belittle the value of divine grace (as the Pelagians did); but rather let him follow the proverb, *God helps him who helps himself.*

It is easy from this to see that the Christian life is really nothing other than one long cross and one long prayer. When I say *cross,* understand it of the whole of man with all his powers, for all have been crippled by sin, and all need the touch of reforming steel. Thus there must be a cross for the body, and another for the eyes, one for the ears and another for the tongue, one for the affections and sensual appetites, another for the imagination.

All these crosses are necessary. The pain and death experienced from the Cross is what our soul should choose and embrace. It is through the Cross that we become dead to the life of the first Adam, so we may live the life of Christ who is the second Adam. Without the Cross, our prayers are of no value, except to plunge us deeper into error. Toil avails us nothing without prayer, since it achieves nothing durable, and prayer without toil is profitless, since it bears no fruit.

With these two qualifications we shall become the living temple of God, for he has two sanctuaries: the one of *sacrifice,*[3] the other of *prayer.*[4] With these we shall go to *the mountain of myrrh and the hill of frankincense,*[5] ascending the slopes by way of the sweetness of prayer and the bitterness of mortification.

3. 2 Chr 7:12.

4. Lk 19:46.

5. Song 4:6.